The GROWING SEASON

SARAH PHILPOTT

HARVEST HOUSE PUBLISHERS
EUGENE, OREGON

Cover by Studio Gearbox

Interior design by Chad Dougherty

Cover photo by Brittany Casavant Photography

Cover photo © Route66 / Shutterstock

Interior images © aimintang, cihanterlan, ioanmasay, Tas3 / Gettyimages; AliasLibrarian, aitoff / Pixabay

For bulk, special sales, or ministry purchases, please call 1.800.547.8979.
Email: customerservice@hhpbooks.com

is a federally registered trademark of The Hawkins Children's LLC. Harvest House Publishers, Inc., is the exclusive licensee of the trademark.

The Growing Season

Published by Harvest House Publishers
Eugene, Oregon 97408
www.harvesthousepublishers.com

ISBN 978-0-7369-8278-8 (hardcover)
ISBN 978-0-7369-8279-5 (eBook)

Library of Congress Control Number: 2021935206

Printed in China

21 22 23 24 25 26 27 28 29 / RDS / 10 9 8 7 6 5 4 3 2 1

To the best farm kids in the world:
Titus, Sophie, Beckham, and Stella.
I love you, my darlings. More than you shall ever imagine.

To the most wonderful farmer husband in the world: Perry.
Thank you for making family as much a priority as the land.
You build a heritage all around.

To my farm parents, Doug and Kim;
my farm-in-loves, Dale and Ruthe;
and my farm besties.
Thank you for all the down-on-the-farm
love and support you've gifted me.

But above all,
thank you to our Lord.
For everything is of You and because of You.

CONTENTS

Introduction 7

WINTER

Welcome Winter 11
New Life on the Farm 13
Welcome to the Farmhouse 17
Good Soil on the Farm 21
Light on the Farm 25
Lost on the Farm 29
Winter Wonderland on the Farm 33
Cattle Out! 37
Breaking Ground on the Farm 41

SPRING

Welcome Spring 47
Planting on the Farm 49
Pruning on the Farm 53
Trucks on the Farm 57
Seeds on the Farm 61
Puddles on the Farm 65
Goats on the Farm 69
Bees on the Farm 73
Deep Roots on the Farm 77
Making Hay on the Farm 81
Rambo on the Farm 85
Picnics on the Farm 89
Bursting with Worship on the Farm 93

SUMMER

Welcome Summer 99
Fireflies on the Farm 101

Planting Pumpkins on the Farm . . . 105
Heaven's Dew on the Farm . . . 109
Blooming on the Farm . . . 113
The Fourth on the Farm . . . 117
Wildflowers on the Farm . . . 121
Oh, Deere! . . . 125
Bear on the Farm . . . 131
Corn Shucking on the Farm . . . 135
Getting Away from the Farm . . . 139
Fowl on the Farm . . . 143
Rest on the Farm . . . 147

FALL

Welcome Fall . . . 153
Apple Picking on the Farm . . . 155
Fugitive on the Farm . . . 159
Delayed Harvest on the Farm . . . 163
Letting Go on the Farm . . . 167
Spills on the Farm . . . 171
Pumpkin Party on the Farm . . . 175
Bulls on the Farm . . . 179
Staying Present on the Farm . . . 183
One-Room Schoolhouse on the Farm . . . 187
Ducks on the Farm . . . 191
Blessings on the Farm . . . 195
Thanksgiving on the Farm . . . 199
Royalty on the Farm . . . 203
Christmas Trees on the Farm . . . 207
Nativity on the Farm . . . 211
Fallow Pasture on the Farm . . . 215
Notes . . . 220
Thanks, Y'all . . . 222

Introduction

Hi, friend. It's so nice to meet you. I'm Sarah—farm gal, farm wife, and farm mom. I don't claim to be a real-deal farmer like my husband, but I do get to sit shotgun in his tractor and watch this world of God's whirl.

I hope this book will take you down memory lane or give you a reflection of what life is like in your neck of the woods. Or perhaps farm life seems distant from your current life, but you are intrigued by a place where the sign of a good day is when your boots get a little muddy.

Whether or not your home looks like mine, I wrote this book for me and for you. To help us both stay focused on God and grow in Him. He is the ultimate farmer. To Him we owe everything.

I like to watch the happenings of the farm and relate it to what God says in the Bible. This devotional is a little year-long glimpse into our Tennessee farm life, designed to encourage you and draw you closer to Him as you learn about the land. Are all farms and ranches the same? No way! Our farm experience is vastly different from that of the dairy farm down the road, the chicken farm across the state, the corn farm out in the heartland, the ranch out west, and the pumpkin patch off the Pacific Coast Highway. Farms and ranches are unique and varied. Perhaps what unites us is our love of the land and our recognition that we're part of the greater world.

As you read this book, you'll see statements like, "It's time for *us* to plow the land." Now, I'm not out there driving the tractor for that plow. I'm the one doing the farm philosophizing. I do love planting pumpkins, harvesting sweet corn, and helping catch baby calves, but I don't consider myself a true-blue farmer. I'm learning as I go.

I designed this book so each week you can read a seasonal devotion—some humorous, some contemplative. Some include recipes, some include journal tasks, and some include tips from my husband, Farmer Perry. I hope they encourage you in your day, make you savor the simple, or at least give you a chuckle.

Each season begins with a welcome page where we plot our intentions. Seasonally we will reflect on what we can plant in our lives, what we can cultivate in our lives, what we can prune from our lives, and what scripture we can meditate upon.

I'm elated you are here for this little adventure down on the farm! Thank you for coming out to the country. We are excited to have you visit.

WINTER

Welcome Winter

To appreciate the beauty of a snowflake it is
necessary to stand out in the cold.

ARISTOTLE

Smell the crispness of the air? See the gray skies heralding snow? Taste the hot cocoa? Hear the wind blowing through the trees? The weather is mighty cold, but there is beauty all around.

On the farm we have lots of winter tasks. Each day is different, but some of our farm goals for the season include...

- feeding cattle each day
- mending fences and cleaning fencerows
- checking for baby calves
- fixing equipment
- getting the ground ready for spring planting
- chopping wood for the fireplace
- ordering seed
- pruning

Farm gal, while we prepare the land, how about we also spend time readying our souls for the new year? Let's make a list of our intentions. We can spend some time this week scribbling out our thoughts. Of course, just like on a farm,

plans change. It's okay if our intentions don't all garner check marks. The best-laid plans often go awry, as the poet Robert Burns noted. Let's enjoy the ride!

What might you like to…

- *plant in your life?* What can you sow?
- *cultivate in your life?* What can you tend to that's already growing?
- *prune in your life?* What do you need to discard or trim a bit?

PICK A SCRIPTURE

What scripture can you meditate on for the winter season?

PRAY A PRAYER

Heavenly Father, may we take time to play in the snowflakes and look up to You, the provider of our very lives.

JANUARY

New Life on the Farm

God said, "Let us make man in our image, after our likeness. And let them have dominion over the fish of the sea and over the birds of the heavens and over the livestock and over all the earth and over every creeping thing that creeps on the earth."

GENESIS 1:26

Down here on our farm the newness of the year brings forth the newness of life. Winter is the season when our baby calves take their first breaths, take in their first milk, and take their first steps.

Sounds sublime, doesn't it?

January, February, and March are known as "calving season" for us. My husband, Perry, and our farm workers daily drive through pastures to see if any newborn calves can be spied lying in the grass. These calves must be located so we can check their health, ensure the mama is taking care of her offspring, and make sure predators are kept at bay.

We must also check to see if any mamas are having trouble with birthing and need a helping hand. No matter the time of day and no matter the weather, caring for our herds is our chief concern. We are privileged to live out this Genesis 1:26 calling of caretaking.

Hundreds of calves are born on our farm each calving season. Our goal is to welcome these sweets in an easy manner. We want our calves to be born gently to conscientious mamas. We also want to ensure no coyotes enter the fields.

That's our perfect-world plan. But we don't live in a perfect world, do we? Plans go haywire. A mama might have trouble with the birthing process, and

Perry will need to help deliver a calf when he and I were supposed to be on a date. Or coyotes will come into the pasture in the middle of the night. Or a mama doesn't completely care for her calf, and we have to take it to the barn to bottle-feed. Vultures even try to hurt the calves. Anything can happen! We must stay watchful.

The only thing to expect on a farm is the unexpected, and we try our best to embrace the spirit of adventure and adaptability.

One frigid and frosty morning, Perry and Jackie, our chief foreman, loaded into the feed truck and set off through the pastures to check for new calves and make sure the cattle had plenty of hay. As they glanced across the field they saw a cow, off by herself, standing at the edge of the creek. That cow was gazing into the water and not paying a bit of attention to the new shipment of hay.

Red flag.

Perry and Jackie hightailed it to the creek. There, in the ice-cold water, was a newborn calf. Bobbing her head and sinking deeper into the murk. Seconds from certain death.

Apparently the mama cow had given birth by the creek bed, and the calf had rolled down into the water. The mama had no way to retrieve her newborn. So she stood there, watching.

Now polar bear plunges, where folks choose to jump into frigid waters, are all the rage across the world for thrill seekers. In fact, it's a New Year's tradition for many who love a frosty welcome to the year. But Perry didn't wake up that morning hankering for an ice bath. In fact, he'd dressed in his Carhartt overalls with the aspiration of staying dry. But a polar dip was where the day led. So Perry jumped, fully clothed, into that creek and picked up that half-drowned calf.

He wrapped the babe in his jacket, dried it off, carried it up the creek bank, and nestled it against its mama. He and Jackie then grabbed some hay and made a bed for them right in the middle of that pasture. The calf started sucking its mama's warm milk, the mama started licking the wet calf, and all was right in the world again.

It's situations like this that require adaptability (and a quick trip to the farmhouse for a dry pair of clothes!). Adapting can be hard, can't it? We might have a goal in mind, but getting to that endpoint can take a million twists and turns.

Farm gal, we can either get angry when life doesn't go according to our plans, or we can focus on our overarching, God-given directives.

At the dawn of the new year we often create resolutions for ourselves. But within this goal-setting process we must stay alert to the needs directly in front of us. Even if that means an occasional polar plunge into the creek.

As we embark upon this new year, let's resolve to *try* to keep our self-made commitments—but let's not get all bent out of shape when things go haywire.

> The heart of man plans his way,
> but the LORD *establishes his steps* (Proverbs 16:9).

Resolutions are good, but resolving to react to the immediate needs God sets in front of us (even when it hinders our "goals") is more important. It is a hard row to hoe, but let's resolve not to get agitated at undone plans when unexpected situations arise. Let's embrace whatever new adventure God sets before us with love, kindness, and a can-do spirit.

Farm gal, it's a fresh year and anything is possible. That's pretty exciting.

GIVE ME SOME SUGAR

My kids and I love bundling up and helping Perry catch baby calves. My two oldest are truly a help, while the rest of us are along for the ride! When we come in from this winter farm adventure, there is nothing better than a cup of hot cocoa to warm our bodies. Homemade, of course.

When your plans go awry, break out the sweet stuff and savor the moment. Hot cocoa makes everything better, doesn't it? Here is my favorite recipe.

Homemade Hot Cocoa

½ cup sugar
¼ cup baking cocoa
Dash of salt
4 cups milk
Splash of vanilla

Mix the dry ingredients and add to the milk. Pour all into a saucepan. While constantly stirring, bring to a rolling boil. Turn down heat, add vanilla, and stir. Pour into four mugs, pass around to your loved ones, and enjoy! Top with marshmallows or whipped cream for an even more indulgent treat!

JANUARY

Welcome to the Farmhouse

Where there are no oxen, the manger is clean,
but abundant crops come by the strength of the ox.

PROVERBS 14:4

Folks tend to romanticize life on the farm. Chickens laying eggs in henhouses. Cattle grazing on verdant fields. Folks sitting on front porches, drinking sweet tea and chatting. But ideals don't always equal reality.

Have you ever laughed at social media posts? Go ahead and search #farmhouselife on Instagram. Like seriously—drop this book and take a scroll. Are you chuckling? Maybe rolling your eyes? Those photos are white and clean, with not a speck of mud in sight. Tickles me to death. And simultaneously jolts me to a bit of jealousy.

Once I was trying to decorate my porch for the new season, and I spied a dead chicken in the front yard. The dog wanted dinner, so he had gone to the henhouse. Then he toted his decaying prize to the front yard. I paused my decorating, took the dead chicken, and threw it over the fence. Can you imagine if I had posted that scene on social media? I'm not sure my photos would inspire #farmhousejealousy in others.

Farmhouse is a word that has two distinct connotations.

In one sense the word conjures up images of homes bedecked with pristine white shiplap, barnwood accents, and perfectly clean mudrooms. Families in those homes gather around the table at a certain time each evening to enjoy a farm-to-table meal. Organic, of course.

But we farm gals know that this vision is false. Totally false. It sits on a bed of HGTV lies. (But I sure do love that shiplap bed, don't you?) We know that a working farmhouse offers floors with straight-from-the-barn footprints and mudrooms full of mud. *Pristine* is not in our vocabulary—unless we are talking about the antique milk glass sitting in the hutch. Our families gather in the fields during the harvest season for a meal of ham sandwiches. And, on occasion, we find a dead, rotting animal in our front yard. This, my friends, is a true farmhouse.

I petition that no one should be able describe their home as a farmhouse unless they've had a genuine farmer walk through the kitchen in mud-caked boots. Bonus points for not scolding him because he's had a hard day and truly just wanted a hug and kiss.

Once a friend walked into my home for the first time and remarked, "It's like *Fixer Upper*, but more lived in." I giggled. Yes, it is certainly more lived in. And although I feel like I labor in vain trying to keep the floors swept and the laundry clean, I certainly love it out here in the country.

But there is nothing easy about being a farm gal, is there? This life brings extra blessings, but along with those blessings come extra mess, extra vacuuming, and extra mopping. We've all got the proverbial dead chicken in our yards.

This verse helps me stay sane: "Where there are no oxen, the manger is clean, but abundant crops come by the strength of the ox" (Proverbs 14:4). This reminder encourages me to practice gratitude for the hard circumstances, the toilsome labor, and the straight-up yucky (someone has to clean up the muck the oxen leave in the manger).

Let's break down that verse. If we reverse the phrasing, we see that a manger is clean if it has no oxen. Simply put, a manger is clean if the barn is empty of life.

I don't know about you, but that puts things in perspective for me. If I applied that concept to my house, it would mean "a house is clean if it has no people." I'd rather have the people, wouldn't you? A few hours of solitude is absolute bliss, but I wouldn't sacrifice a lifetime of community for a perpetually pristine house.

I'm happy that God has allowed my home to be full of littles and a husband. I'll take the #farmhousemess, because it means I have a crop of love inside my home and am blessed to be a caretaker for our earth. Instead of jealousy, I will practice gratitude.

What are your manger blessings? I bet you've got a ton too. So farm gal, let's choose not to be jealous or filled with a sense of inadequacy if our homes don't always resemble the ones shared with #farmhouselife. Instead, let's look at those posts as images of beautiful art and simultaneously realize that our real lives are equally beautiful.

BLESS THE MESS CHALLENGE

How can you praise God for the mess? Let's consider our own "farmhouse mess" blessings. This exercise will help retrain our minds to lean toward gratitude.

Write out Proverbs 14:4 on a piece of paper and start a list of manger blessings. For example:

- the laundry pile (I have a family to love)
- the dust on the floor (I have people walking in my home)
- the car that needs gas (I have transportation, places to go, and people to see)

Tape this list to the wall of your laundry room, above your kitchen sink, or in your mudroom. Gaze at it often so you can see the blessing in the mess.

Father, sometimes it is hard to be a caretaker, but You have given us this important calling from the advent of time. Let my eyes see the mess in my manger as evidence that I am blessed with an abundant crop. (Also, please help me not to yell at my family when they walk in with mud-caked boots.) When I'm worn out, please provide me the energy to keep going. Father, thank You for my greatest blessing: I have Jesus Christ, who frees me from the ultimate mess in my life—sin. Amen.

JANUARY

Good Soil on the Farm

Some fell into good soil and grew and yielded a hundredfold.

LUKE 8:8

The new year not only lends itself to goals, but also to times of reflecting. Have you thought much about your previous year or the last decade of your life? Go ahead and meander down those memories.

Do you ever wish you could bury some of the recollections that pop into your head? Me too! Some of our memories are sad, some downright embarrassing, and some icky. And most of the *bad* we would characterize as *useless*. But God wastes nothing. What we think of as bad, God can help us use for good.

Let's take this topic to the farm. I'll set the scene.

My days are often spent inside with my little ones. Often, we end up at our farmhouse table. On this recent January morning, the golden sunshine spilled inside through the windows, causing my gaze to look outward.

I looked across the front yard, past our small vineyard and the pasture that houses our horse, llamas, and duck pond, and saw—way, way across the distance, right where the sun rises—the pasture where we grow our pumpkins and sweet corn. It's not a big field, just a few acres. There, humming along in that field, was the old red Massey Ferguson tractor. The red coloring seemed extra vibrant in that field where winter had subdued the color of the grass. The tractor, and the farmhand driving that tractor, were working on the soil.

It sounds like a beautiful scene, doesn't it? Sunshine. Tractor. Farmland. A vision created for a cup of coffee and quiet reflection. Pure goodness of a morning.

But you know what was being pulled behind that tractor? A spreader.

A manure spreader, to be exact.

You know that smell. There I was, adoringly gazing at manure being scattered across the field. *Organic amendment* is the formal way to describe what was going into the ground. But we all know manure is manure, even with a gussied-up name.

My reaction to the scene was laughable. But it did get me thinking about bad being used for good. The fertilization of fields is one way to promote good soil. And good soil is pivotal for crop growth.

On our farm, the cattle refuse from the barns is loaded into the manure spreader. Then the spreader disperses the manure on the cropland. The waste is literally used for growth.

Isn't it amazing how God created even the waste of the animals for the good of the earth? That manure is spread across the field in the winter; microbes break down the substance over time; and come spring the nutrients of nitrogen, phosphorus, and potassium from the waste will have completely mixed with the earth, making the soil a rich environment for our sweet corn. Yes, the yucky and the good mix and mingle to create a place of growth. What we often think of as waste, God uses for good.

Farm gal, this isn't just true of our fields, but of our spiritual lives as well. Those things we reflect upon as bad from the previous year? God can use all of that as a springboard for growth. Our bad experiences can help us build empathy or endurance. Our trials can help us increase our patience, gratitude, and ability to forgive. What you view as waste from your previous year can be an opportunity for growth.

Of course, God must be in this mix. Absent of Him, growth would never occur.

> God is within her, she will not fall (Psalm 46:5 NIV).

Friend, God redeems the icky parts of our life and turns them into spiritual growth. We only need accept Him as our master farmer.

SOIL TO SOUL CHALLENGE

Will you set aside an hour of time to cultivate your soul? Gather these supplies: paper, pen, pot for a plant, soil, and a small plant or seeds.

On the piece of paper write some memories that stand out from the previous year. Some of these memories will cause you to laugh. Some of these memories will cause you to cringe. But no matter the emotion, write the memory. Your handwriting doesn't have to be pretty. Your spelling doesn't have to be correct. Just write out your thoughts.

After, tear up the paper and put the pieces in a pile in front of you. Let the good memories mix with the bad memories. Pray to God that He will help you use *all* these experiences to grow in Him.

Now, place those strips of paper in the bottom of the pot. Cover them with soil and plant the plant or seeds. In the coming days, cultivate the new life with water and sunshine and watch it grow. As you watch, stay mindful that this sprout comes forth from the culmination of all your experiences: the good and the bad.

You can modify this challenge any way you choose. Perhaps you would prefer to take your strips of paper and mix them underneath a rosebush you already have in your garden. Or you could place the scraps of memories under a vegetable crop. However you approach this activity, it should help your soul understand that God wastes nothing.

JANUARY

Light on the Farm

You are the light of the world. A city set on a hill cannot be hidden. Nor do people light a lamp and put it under a basket, but on a stand, and it gives light to all in the house.

MATTHEW 5:14-15

There my son stood, teeth chattering, in our living room. With soaking coveralls, he was iced to the bone by the January temperatures.

I'd sent my Titus, then seven or eight, to gather wood from the woodshed so we could keep the fire in our fireplace going. But he'd gotten a bit sidetracked by wanting to "test the frozen pond" (a goldfish pond) and fallen straight through. He'd walked back to our house with no wood, just dripping water. I got him into the warmth of a shower and decided his near hypothermic state was lesson enough on thin ice.

Wood fireplaces are so cozy. In our home, the first coldish day in November is greeted with a roaring fire. But fires take effort—it's not easy to keep one going, or even to get it started.

I wonder if the wood fireplace will start dying off as a desired feature in homes. People love automation. But you can't tell an electronic device to "light up the wood fire!" Nope. A real fire takes work, time, and attention. You must chop the wood, stack the wood, and carry the wood into the house.

And then you have to get the thing lit. Which isn't as easy as it sounds. You must patiently layer the fire, keep it stoked, and add wood. Which means more trips to the woodshed—where your wood retriever is liable to fall into a pond.

Oh, and the ashes. Those must be gathered from the hearth. Then the floor must be swept because, of course, ashes will escape the bucket.

It sounds like I'm complaining, doesn't it? I promise I'm not. I'm just pointing out that fire making is a tad labor intensive. But the warm payoff is worth the toil; a fire is delightful.

CHOPPING WOOD

I learned from my grandfather that it is best to chop wood during the waning moon. During this moon phase, right after the full moon, the sap is supposedly down toward the root of the trees. This makes the wood cure quicker and burn longer. Is this scientific? I'm not sure. But this old-timer knowledge seems to work.

During biblical times, fire wasn't just about ambience; it was a necessity. For cooking. For warmth. For being able to see in the darkness. Clay lamps, fueled by olive oil, were utilized when day turned to night. And hearths were kept aglow so food could be prepared.

Imagine having your very survival and quality of life dependent upon keeping a fire going at all times. People couldn't neglect the flame.

But you know what? We aren't supposed to neglect our internal flame either.

In the New Testament, Jesus instructs us, "You are the light of the world. A city set on a hill cannot be hidden. Nor do people light a lamp and put it under a basket, but on a stand, and it gives light to all in the house" (Matthew 5:14-15).

Putting the light under a basket would be absurd. A hidden light is not going to cut it. As we say in the South, "That dog won't hunt." Likewise, Christ says that it's absurd for us to have His light within us and keep that light hidden.

We were designed to illuminate the world with the light of Christ. Our good works and kindness and Christian attributes point folks to the power source of our internal light—God. Good works aren't our salvation, but they are part of our evangelism. These lights shouldn't be hidden.

It can sometimes be exhausting to engage in Christlike goodness. Just as keeping a physical fire going takes effort, so too must effort be devoted to keeping our internal lights shining. We can easily be distracted (like my son at the goldfish pond), and we can easily decide that the work isn't worth the payoff (but oh, think of the joy of a warm fire!). Yes, good works and showing kindness and growing in holiness all take effort, but the payoff is life giving.

Think about the last time you sat around a campfire. What did everyone do? Folks tend to gaze into the sparkling flames with wonder and peace, don't they? It's quite amazing to think that we, as God's creations, can be that light. For when others come across our path, they might look at us and experience the wonder and peace of God. It's not us they see—but the power of Christ. He is the source of peace and eternal salvation.

Let's go out into the world and shine. Not hiding the light. Not allowing the light to wane. But gifting others the light of Christ.

WOOD TO CHOP

As the saying goes, we've all got a little wood to chop. Take inventory of your spiritual life and identify a few things you can do to stoke your fire. Spending more time in the Bible or in prayer and praise can help you get that light shining stronger.

Talk with God and identify how you can do a better job making sure His light is put on a stand and not under a basket. Then put in the effort to pile some logs on the fire, so your light will blaze, and others will see His glory.

FEBRUARY

Lost on the Farm

The Son of Man came to seek and to save the lost.

LUKE 19:10

It's bedtime, the sky is dark, and quietness surrounds us. My husband opens the front door and walks outside, like he does most nights.

I used to think Perry was reveling in the beauty of the stars. And that he does. He loves to find constellations. However, I also know he has another motive for stepping outside.

He's listening.

Did you know that a mama cow bellows when in distress? Our calves are young. Although their mamas keep them close, perilous situations do occur. Especially in the midst of calving season. Coyotes lurk and come out of their forest homes during the night. These beautiful but dangerous predators know pastures house their prey. So my husband and our neighbors are vigilant.

That is why Perry is on the porch. He's listening for the howls of the coyotes and the bellows of mama cows.

On many nights he comes back inside to slip into bed. But on other eves, when he senses distress, he grabs the keys to his truck, along with his rifle, and heads to the fields. He searches to save the one.

Now and again his searching leads him to find a lost calf that has fallen into a sinkhole, perhaps running from a coyote. Other times he finds a calf about to lose its life to the circling predators.

Saving those calves is the mission of the night. This is his duty as a farmer and rancher.

You see, the lost and distressed are valuable. They are part of his herd.

His herd.

Farm gal, our Father in heaven does the same for us and so much more. He is constantly monitoring, ceaselessly looking, and always willing to come swoop us up and wrap us in His safety.

We are valuable. When we are lost, He seeks us and saves us. When we are distressed, He hears our bellows. When we are in danger, we can trust He will walk beside us.

My husband, the farmer, is a mere mortal and can't save every distressed calf, although he tries his hardest. But our Father in heaven never fails. He loves each and every one of us and has the power to save those of us who call on Him. He loves us. Whether we are in distress, covered with the mire of sin, or in a figurative sinkhole, He always comes to our rescue with the offer of saving us. He doesn't even have to grab his truck keys or head to the pasture; He is always with us.

Luke 19 tells the account of Zacchaeus. Remember singing about him as children? I'll never forget those hand motions from my days at Double Springs Baptist. Zacchaeus, as you will recall, was a tax collector who climbed into a sycamore tree to get a look at Jesus. But what the children's song fails to tell us is that many in the crowd thought Zacchaeus to be unworthy of Jesus' attention. Zacchaeus was dismissed by many of the crowd as a lost rich man with no value to the kingdom of heaven or to Jesus. Why would Jesus care about him? He was nothing more than a sinner.

Sometimes we feel we are of no value to Jesus. Perhaps we don't think of ourselves as worthless or lost, but all of us, at some time or another, have experienced a waning confidence and have questioned our innate value to Jesus. Perhaps because of our sin. Or perhaps because of our position (lowly or high).

But we, just like Zacchaeus, are worthy to our Lord. That's what Zacchaeus' story tells us. It reminds us that we are all worthy, welcomed, and loved—because Jesus sought out that sinful tax collector in the sycamore tree.

Zacchaeus was literally looking for the Lord, and the Lord said something to the effect of "Come on down!" (see Luke 19:5). Jesus told this man and all those around him (who were probably looking at this situation with high skepticism), "Today salvation has come to this house, since he also is a son of Abraham. For the Son of Man came to seek and to save the lost" (verses 9-10).

Our Jesus seeks and saves.

Yes, farm gal, we are all worthy. Jesus is in the business of seeking the lost and distressed. We are in His herd, and He will never fail us. Our Father always listens.

Let's call on Him always and forever, accept His love, and give thanks for His unwavering mission of saving the lost.

Heavenly Father, thank You so much for looking out for me. Thank You for listening to my every plea. For hearing my every bellow. And for taking notice of my every word. Thank You for always coming to my rescue and making known to me that I am worthy and belong to You. With You, I am never lost. Amen.

HAVE YOU EATEN YET?

Jesus invited Himself over to Zacchaeus' house; I wonder what Zacchaeus served Him. If Jesus came to my house, He'd probably get hearty beef stew. As cattle farmers, our freezer is always stocked with beef! Here is a stew to have on the stovetop if you are expecting a visitor or feeding your family. You can even make this, then freeze it and thaw to eat later.

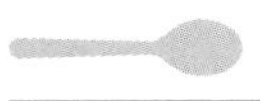

Hearty Beef Stew

- 1 T. vegetable oil
- Beef stew meat (around 2 lb.)
- ⅓ cup chopped onion
- 1 cup diced celery
- 1 cup sliced carrots
- 1 can (15 oz.) corn

- 1 cup diced potatoes
- 4 tsp. salt
- Dash of pepper
- 1 can (28 oz.) whole, peeled tomatoes
- 16 oz. tomato juice
- 6 cups of water or beef stock
- 2 tsp. Worcestershire sauce
- ¼ tsp. chili powder
- 2 bay leaves

Heat the oil over medium heat in a large pot or Dutch oven. Add the beef and sauté until seared (around 10 minutes). Remove the beef and put aside. Sauté the vegetables in the pot you used to sauté the beef. Sauté until the vegetables are soft (around 5 minutes). Add the sautéed beef back to the vegetables. Season the beef and vegetables with salt and pepper. Then add the remainder of ingredients in with the beef and vegetables. Bring to a boil. Reduce heat to low and simmer until the meat is tender. I like to let mine simmer on the stove for at least 2 to 3 hours. Enjoy!

FEBRUARY

Winter Wonderland on the Farm

He spreads the snow like wool
and scatters the frost like ashes.
He hurls down his hail like pebbles.
Who can withstand his icy blast?
He sends his word and melts them;
he stirs up his breezes, and the waters flow.

PSALM 147:16-18 NIV

Here in Tennessee the excitement of snow rivals that of Christmas morning. We cheer this rare gift from the sky and marvel at the white enchantment. Any amount (even a quarter of an inch) is counted as pure joy. What you might call a light dusting, we refer to as God's favor.

When snow is on the horizon, we immediately commence our peculiar traditions (in between feeding the livestock and other chores, of course). Here are a few examples of how we react to snow around this part of the country.

- Legend suggests that if a large number of children wear their pajamas *inside out* to bed, they will awaken to a winter wonderland. At least that's what elementary teachers preach to the kids when snow is in the forecast. Hey...God works in mysterious ways!
- Similar folklore suggests that *flushing ice cubes* down the toilet will also cause a snow day. (It's better than fishing plastic dinosaurs out of the plumbing, for sure!)
- A proper definition of *snow day* is when school is called off due to

inclement weather. But no snow has to exist on the ground here for school to be canceled—there just has to be the threat of snow. This baffles our northern friends who know that their yoga class isn't even canceled for less than six feet of snow.

- Milk and bread are an absolute necessity if snow is impending. Why? Who knows? But you'll find that if the meteorologist merely utters the word "snow," grocery stores, gas stations, and Dollar Generals in the South will be sold out of this dairy-grain combo within hours. Some theorists refer to this as a financial conspiracy between weathermen and grocery stores.
- Snow cream. Sweet, wonderful snow cream. Although we would never allow our children to drink rainwater by the cupful, we encourage all members of our family to savor this delicious dish of snow scraped from the front yard and carefully mixed with sugar, milk, and vanilla. It is a heavenly treat.
- When a storm arrives, national network television is constantly interrupted so local news stations can provide up-to-the-minute insight on how locals are being affected by the inch of snow that has fallen. Camera crews and news anchors are stationed throughout the area, showcasing the slight dusting on the roads and parking lots.
- All responsible news media utter, "It's treacherous. Don't go out unless you must!" throughout the broadcast. But we do go out. Why? Because snow is so scarce for us that we must experience it. And, of course, test out the tires on our vehicles.
- We pull out clothes from boxes and seldom-used drawers. We dress our kids in a hodgepodge of hand-me-downs so they don't get too frigid. Garbage bags taped over normal footwear can be used for makeshift boots if proper waterproof footwear is not found. It is common for our gloves not to match.

- Snowmen must be built. No matter how pitiful the size, they always look splendid adorned with carrots, coal, and stray sticks.
- Snow might barely cover the grass, but kids and adults alike find a way to sled. And roll in the snow. And make snow angels. And catch snowflakes on their tongues. And pitch snowballs. And wear big, goofy grins on their faces all day. Perfectly content in the fun.
- There is always that one adult who says, "Hey! I'm gonna hook up the four-wheeler / UTV / lawn mower to the sled / inner tube / car hood. Let's show these kids a good time." The kids quickly determine who the responsible (not fun) and irresponsible (super fun) adults are in the group—and they always side with those in the negligent camp. This is precisely why hospitals can't close for a snow day.
- Folks eventually become worn out or freeze and go home for hot cocoa and cookies. In the evening they gather around the table for grilled cheese sandwiches and tomato soup or homemade chili.
- Those who sled on a farm wake up the next morning with bruises from sledding over the ski jumps (frozen manure piles covered in snow) that dotted the pasture.
- When the snow melts, everyone starts praying all over again for another sacred snow day. Because when magic falls from the sky, the world stops, and lifelong memories are made.

Our Southern traditions might seem peculiar to some, but I consider them a celebration of this elusive-to-us miracle. All in all, our strange customs are just a dance of praise to our God. Psalm 19:1 says, "The heavens declare the glory of God, and the sky above proclaims his handiwork." There is no denying that when it snows, we all see the magnificent work of His hands. It is not magic or enchantments that cause the snow—we know that this is a gift from our Creator. A gift we celebrate with all types of revelry.

Thank You, Father, for designing nature as a delight. May I find joy in Your handiwork. As I play in the snow, pick up shells on the beach, or gaze at the rainbow You send after a rainstorm, let me never forget that You create the majesty. You spread the snow. You send Your word and cause the ocean breeze to blow. You paint the rainbow. Thank You, Lord. Amen.

DOWN-HOME PRAISE

Farm gal, celebrate God's gift of snow and make some snow cream! Keep your pantry stocked with sweetened condensed milk so you are ready when the white stuff starts falling.

Snow Cream

- 8 cups fresh snow
- 1 tsp. vanilla
- 1 can (10 oz.) sweetened condensed milk (or you can dissolve ⅓ cup sugar in 1 cup fresh milk)

Put fresh snow in a mixing bowl. Add vanilla. Drizzle sweetened condensed milk on the snow. Mix. Enjoy!

FEBRUARY

Cattle Out!

Let us not grow weary of doing good, for in due season we will reap, if we do not give up.

GALATIANS 6:9

Cattle out. That's what my kids wrote on the tardy slip when they arrived late to school yesterday. They'd woken up and hopped in the pickup with their dad. (He's their morning chauffeur.) But on the drive to school, he got a call that some cattle were on the loose. Quickly assessing the situation, Perry determined that the possibility of someone getting into a car accident due to the cattle being out was worse than a tardy slip for our children. So he turned that truck around and went to handle the cattle gone AWOL. Hence, our children were late to school due to a bovine escape.

Farmers are always on call. It sure does take grit, determination, and hard work to survive out here. Manual labor, with eternally calloused hands, is just part of the gig. So are midnight awakenings and having to jump up from the dinner table mid-bite to put out whatever fire is burning (in both the literal and figurative senses).

My kids watch their daddy put family first, but they also see how he carefully balances this with the reality that farm folks have a duty to their land and animals. This means that if he gets a call that the cattle are out, he must stop, drop whatever he is doing, and roll with the punches. He might miss a basketball game (or two or three).

You see, even though we have great fencing, every now and then a heifer will try for greener pastures. Or someone might forget to shut the gate, and the cows will make their break. We've even had poachers cut our barbed wire.

My mother-in-law, Ruthe, likes to tell a story of when my husband was a little boy. She told him he needed to *shut the barn door*, meaning to zip up his Wranglers. But he took her words literally and hightailed it outside, thinking he needed to jet to the barn and shut the gate so cattle wouldn't escape. From a young age he had learned to have a sense of responsibility to the farm.

Thankfully, he also realized that family was important, and he learned this careful balance that is hard for many farm families. Take, for instance, the night of our wedding. After our wedding ceremony and celebration, we headed to our new home. The next day we were flying to the Caribbean for our honeymoon. But our first night as a married couple was spent in the little farmhouse we'd fixed up.

It was past midnight when we arrived at that little white house down in the valley. And there to greet us was a Black Angus bull. Standing right in the middle of our driveway, staring at us. A standoff.

My husband silently weighed his options. Thankfully, he made the first best decision of our marriage. He drove around the bull, opened the door on my side of the truck, and carried me over the threshold to our home. I'm not sure if our marriage would have kicked off to a great start had he asked his bride, still in her wedding dress, to help put up a 2,000-pound bull. Instead, he waited until I fell asleep and then went out to get the bull back where it belonged.

Does a farm run a person or does a person run a farm? Henry David Thoreau, a great philosopher and writer, offered this humorously accurate statement: "I would say to my fellows, once for all, as long as possible live free and uncommitted. It makes but little difference whether you are committed to a farm or the county jail."[1]

The work on a farm—whether it involves the cattle getting out, problems with wildlife getting into our crops, tractor failure, or flooding—is constant. At times we feel married to our farm or even, as Thoreau suggests, jailed by it.

Interruptions are an expected part of the gig. And we who love our farmers or work side by side with them also learn to roll with the punches. Even if it means arriving late to many events or having to cancel plans because of a farm emergency. Farming is a lifestyle, not just a job.

Stewardship, of home and herd, is why we do it. We are stewards of our farm and land.

Stewardship means "the careful and responsible management of something entrusted to one's care."[2] This farm, and all it encompasses, has been entrusted to us.

We are all stewards of something. Stewards of our home. Stewards of our family. Stewards of God's land. And most importantly, stewards of God's Word.

THAT'S A LONG ROW TO HOE

Sometimes, just like handling the responsibility of life out on a farm, stewardship can bring about challenges. It can cause us to go against our natural feelings, where we want to put self first. Farm gal, you might not be getting up in the middle of night to put up cows, but you might be up helping console your children or taking care of a loved one or finishing an important project. When this happens, pause, redirect thoughts that might lean toward grumpiness, and pray.

Thank You, Lord, for entrusting me with this duty. I pray that I will not grow weary of doing good and I will not give up. It is an honor to be able to care for what You have created. It is an honor to be a steward for You. Amen.

FEBRUARY

Breaking Ground on the Farm

This is what the Lord says to the people
of Judah and to Jerusalem:
"Break up your unplowed ground
and do not sow among thorns."

JEREMIAH 4:3 NIV

Ripper. Pretty harsh-sounding word, right? It can mean a killer who mutilates with a knife. But when Perry says, "Charlee's out in the field with the ripper," he doesn't mean our farm help is in the crop field being stabbed by a murderer. Hold the phone, there is no need to call 911. The only thing being cut up in the field is the soil.

In farm talk a ripper is a plow-like device pulled behind a tractor. The ripper has sharp blades that are used to break up the soil. The victim of the ripper is the hard, compacted earth. This is groundwork that must be done before planting.

Our croplands are fairly free of weeds. One reason is because we employ crop rotation. Take the corn field. After the corn harvest concludes in the fall, we plant winter wheat on this plot of cropland. Not only is this a food source for our cattle, but it also keeps the earth from washing away—erosion is not a good thing!

Plus, it adds much-needed nutrients to the soil. Once the wheat grows a bit, we put the cattle out on that cropland. The cattle chow down on the winter wheat and, by consequence, fertilize the field.

Come early winter of the new year, we relocate the cattle in that pasture to a new field. While the herd grazes somewhere else, the winter wheat in that corn field is left to grow. In early spring the winter wheat is harvested, still green, and we make silage. This silage is stored for the cattle to eat the following winter.

Whew. Lot of work for those acres!

Right now, the field is empty. Fallow. The winter wheat has just been harvested. The cattle are grazing in another pasture. And the farmer is preparing to plant corn again.

But we must pause. Before those corn seeds go in the ground, we must decide whether the soil is good enough to host a crop of corn.

The farmer goes out into the cropland and takes a gander at the soil. Sometimes a soil sample is taken. If the soil is deemed worthy, the next step is planting. But if it's been a particularly wet winter, a hardpan might have developed under our east Tennessee topsoil. This hard layer doesn't let water in and inhibits the growth of seeds. We can't have that. Why would we plant seeds in ground that isn't conducive to growth? So, out comes the ripper. The instrument of breaking.

The ripper is hitched up to the 7810 John Deere tractor, and they're taken into the field. To cut the soil. To soften the ground so water can get into the soil. To ensure that the roots of future plants can grow deep and strong.

We know that under favorable conditions a seed will be able to grow and bear fruit. And that's our goal—to make sure our corn seeds will grow and prosper. To reach this goal we must break up the harsh ground with the sharp blades of the ripper. Otherwise the briars and thorns will take advantage of the barren field and start to flourish. And, as my father-in-law would say, "Ain't no money in briars."

Briars have little value. We desire a field of goodness, not a field of weeds.

Farm gal, we are described as God's field (1 Corinthians 3:9). And God doesn't want us to be full of spiritual weeds, briars, or thorns. Because then His Word cannot grow in our hearts.

Charles Spurgeon posits that the weeds we see in the land were actually created by God for a distinct purpose. He writes, "Are not all thorns and thistles meant to be teachers to sinful men? Are they not brought forth of the earth on purpose that they may show us what sin has done, and the kind of produce that will come when we sow the seed of rebellion against God?"[1]

I see on our farm what happens when thorns and weeds are not eliminated: They take over and choke out the good.

This can happen in our personal lives as well. So, just like the farmer guards and takes care of his soil by turning over the earth, we also must guard and take care of our souls. James 1:21 (NLT) instructs us, "Get rid of all the filth and evil in your lives, and humbly accept the word God has planted in your hearts, for it has the power to save your souls."

God gives us free will. We can choose to let the weeds of sin overtake our hearts, or we can follow God's intent and get rid of the filth. We have the spiritual charge of plowing our hearts so that the implanted Word can flourish.

Jeremiah 4:3 (NIV) says, "This is what the LORD says to the people of Judah and to Jerusalem: 'Break up your unplowed ground and do not sow among thorns.'" God's command wasn't gentle; the plow is sharp. We must break up our unplowed souls.

My husband takes a look at the soil in our cropland. He evaluates what needs to be accomplished and takes the necessary steps. Sometimes that means the ripper gets to ripping. But then the plants can get to growing. And that's a beautiful thing.

Friend, we must take a good look at what is going on in our lives. We are God's field (1 Corinthians 3:9). We are His creation (Ephesians 2:10). He wants us to bloom and prosper. To bloom and prosper, we must evaluate our current state and take necessary steps. We must rip that sin out of our lives so it doesn't spread and choke out all the goodness God has planted within our hearts.

In modern society many are disconnected from the field. Many don't get their hands dirty and feel the weeds between their fingers. They don't realize the constant battle and the plowing that must occur.

Today, spend some time standing back and taking a look at your life. What brambles have overtaken your field? Take the hard step of ripping them out of your life so goodness can get into those crevices. You were created to bloom.

Sometimes that means taking this hard step of pulling up weeds so God's good Word planted within your heart can grow.

Sometimes harmful things try to get into our souls. Let's pluck them out and let sweetness break through.

MADDER THAN A HORNET

My mom once made a chocolate pie full of wasps and sent it with my dad to his workplace. It's now a family legacy. She didn't mean to send a pie full of stingers!

What happened? Well, the kitchen window was open while she was whipping up the pie. Unbeknownst to her, when she stepped out of the kitchen wasps flew into the sweet mix.

Everyone raved about the pie at my dad's workplace. But they were curious as to what was so crunchy. Then someone started pulling out the wasps. It is my favorite dessert—sans the wasps, of course!

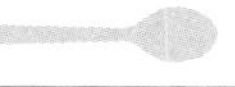

Kim's Wasper Pie

- 12 T. (1½ sticks) butter
- 1 cup sugar
- 3 squares unsweetened chocolate
- 1 tsp. vanilla
- 4 eggs
- 1 baked pie shell
- whipped cream (homemade or prepackaged)

To make the chocolate mousse, first soften the butter at room temperature. Cream the softened butter and sugar. Melt the chocolate over boiling water using a double boiler, and then allow the melted chocolate to cool until it is warm. Stir the cooled chocolate into the creamed mixture. Add vanilla. Add the eggs one at a time, beating the mixture for five minutes after adding each egg. Pour mixture into the pie shell. Top with whipped cream and chill. Enjoy!

SPRING

Welcome Spring

Some old-fashioned things like fresh air
and sunshine are hard to beat.

LAURA INGALLS WILDER

Smell the roses that are in bloom? See the buds forming on the trees? Taste the first bites of the garden produce? Hear the birds chirping? You know what that means: Spring is here! Which means new farm tasks are also in bloom. Some of our spring goals here on the farm include…

- preparing the ground for crops
- sowing grass and forage
- planting crops and the backyard garden
- getting bulls to the fields for breeding
- raising chicks and ducklings
- preparing machinery

Farm gal, just like a seed dwells in the soil, let us dwell in God. Let's spend some time this week scribbling out our thoughts on our spring intentions. Of course, just like on a farm, plans change. It's okay if our intentions don't all garner check marks. The best-laid plans often go awry, as the poet Robert Burns noted. Let's enjoy the ride!

What might you like to...

- *plant in your life?* What can you sow?
- *cultivate in your life?* What can you tend to that's already growing?
- *prune in your life?* What do you need to discard or trim a bit?

PICK A SCRIPTURE

What scripture can you meditate on for the spring season?

PRAY A PRAYER

Heavenly Father, may we stand in the sunshine and breathe in the fresh spring air. May we also dwell in Your goodness and cultivate all the seeds You have planted within our hearts.

MARCH

Planting on the Farm

Other seeds fell on good soil and produced grain,
some a hundredfold, some sixty, some thirty.
He who has ears, let him hear.

MATTHEW 13:8-9

"Planted any corn yet?"

Sit in the Tellico Junction Café in the spring, and you'll hear farm talk from the center table—the place where local farmers sometimes congregate to eat a hot meal and trade stories, jabs, and strategies.

"Getting fifty acres planted today. Lord willing, if the rain holds off, we'll get fifty more tomorrow."

Most all the farmers sitting at that table are in planting season. Fields have been fertilized, ground has been broken, and now seed is being sown—or will be, after they all finish their meals.

In biblical times, planting seeds was a task accomplished by hand. Many farmers carried seeds in a pouch or basket and broadcast them onto plowed ground. Some of us still use this method in our backyard gardens. But the farmers at the Tellico Junction Café aren't sowing seeds by hand. Most own seed planters, which is an implement they pull behind their tractors so they can efficiently plant acres and acres and acres of row crops.

The parable of the sower, found in the Gospels of Matthew, Mark, and Luke, offers Jesus' take on planting. The Bible tells us that Jesus sat in a boat, with onlookers all along the shore who had gathered to listen to His words. Jesus started His story with a farmer scattering seeds. Throwing them; hoping they'd prosper.

But some of the seeds, Jesus explained, didn't make it to the harvest. In countryfolk talk, "They didn't bear nothing."

Some of the seeds were scattered and instantly eaten up by birds. The ground was too hard, and the seeds didn't get into the safety of the soil in time.

Some of the seeds were thrown into rocky areas. They were doomed from the start. Roots can't go deep in rocks, and they can't get to the source of life: water. Jesus says those plants sprang up but then withered in the hot sun.

Some of the seeds fell among the thorns. And those wicked things that poke and prick choked out the plants.

None of those seeds grew into harvestable plants. Poor farmer. All that work for nothing.

But the farmer tried. He persisted. And he wasn't stingy. Every now and then he'd have a seed fall into good soil. And the seeds that fell into that soil produced a good crop. So good, in fact, that the crop multiplied.

Good soil matters, doesn't it? Which is why we take time to baby the soil on our farm. We fertilize it. Make sure it's plowed, tilled, or ripped. And then we do the planting. Even then, with all that work and effort, we can't be assured every single seed will be fruitful. Yet we still sow. And Lord willing, most of the seed will land on good soil and turn into an abundant crop by harvesttime.

The parable of the sower aligns perfectly with agricultural science. But Jesus wasn't sitting in that boat, telling people farm facts. He wasn't encouraging them to go home and get their soil in order. No, the message Jesus wanted the onlookers (and us) to receive pertains to the soul. Read Jesus' explanation of His parable:

> When anyone hears the word of the kingdom and does not understand it, the evil one comes and snatches away what has been sown in his heart. This is what was sown along the path. As for what was sown on rocky ground, this is the one who hears the word and immediately receives it with joy, yet he has no root in himself, but

> endures for a while, and when tribulation or persecution arises on account of the word, immediately he falls away. As for what was sown among thorns, this is the one who hears the word, but the cares of the world and the deceitfulness of riches choke the word, and it proves unfruitful. As for what was sown on good soil, this is the one who hears the word and understands it. He indeed bears fruit and yields, in one case a hundredfold, in another sixty, and in another thirty (Matthew 13:19-23).

Jesus sat in that boat asking people to go from soil to soul.

He says we must have hearts that are softened and ready to receive the Word. Surface level ain't going to cut it; the evil one snatches.

He says our spiritual lives need depth. Persecution will come; if our roots aren't deep enough, we will not survive the scorching trials.

He says we need to be wary of temptation. We must repent of sin that can choke out all the fruit we are capable of bearing through Christ.

Jesus tells us to be a doer and a hearer (see also James 1:22). A believer and a follower. With Him, we will bear fruit.

Farm gal, we must plant the Word of God deep into our souls and care for it. Psalm 92:13 tells us that people who are "planted in the house of the Lord; they flourish in the courts of our God." God is the good soil in which we should plant our lives. Then our lives will be amplified for Him. That's a crop worth sowing!

LEARNING THE WAY OF THE LAND

Take in the knowledge from those you know who have been farming longer than you. Whether it be a grandparent or a farmer down the road, go listen, learn, and watch. The best farming knowledge is passed on from generation to generation.

THROW SOME SEED

One way to throw seed is to encourage folks. Everyone, those you meet in person or those with whom you communicate on social media, feels a bit better by receiving an authentic, biblical boost by another person. Words are powerful. Throw out some kindness today and every day.

❖ MARCH ❖

Pruning on the Farm

I am the true vine, and my Father is the vinedresser. Every branch in me that does not bear fruit he takes away, and every branch that does bear fruit he prunes, that it may bear more fruit.

JOHN 15:1-2

God was bathing us in a sunset as we were taking care of our blackberry vines. We don't have acres and acres of these—only a small section on the east side of our farmhouse. Each June the brambles burst with goodness for us to gift, use to make cobblers, and eat straight from the vine. But today we weren't enjoying the fruit of our labor. Instead, we were laboring so we could have fruit. We held pruning shears in our gloved hands. My oldest helped us with the cutting while the two middles loaded up the discarded branches and placed them in a pile, ready to be taken off to be burned.

As I was cutting, I reflected on doing the same task a year or two back, when I'd first helped my husband prune these blackberries. I'd asked, "Perry, why are we doing this?" He answered, " 'Cause to grow a little, you gotta cut a little."

Boom. I felt like I'd just heard the words of a great philosopher. Except it was my husband bundled up in a Carhartt jacket clipping away, explaining to me that the plants need relief from the weight of the dead.

"The branches," he went on, "need spacin' so air can circulate and sunlight can reach the shoots. Otherwise the fruit is too clustered and dies from darkness. The old branches sit there, not lettin' room for the new. It's the cutting that allows for new growth and a more fruitful bounty."

I felt like new understanding had just reached my soul. This renewal didn't come because I was looking forward to a blackberry cobbler, but because I felt like I'd just received a spiritual answer to an agricultural question.

At that time my own life was dragging from the weight of self-allowed obligations. Too much of everything was crowding my life, and it seemed the best of me was withering. I'd been praying to God for guidance on how to handle a few situations. Should I lessen my obligations? What could I cut?

I bet you can relate. Whether you are single, married, or widowed. Whether you have five kids, one kid, or no kids. I bet you too have felt (or currently feel) the strain of life. If you are like me, you've had many an internal conversation on how you should spend the time God provides you.

At many times in our lives we feel this weight on our souls. Weight from good endeavors and from unworthy endeavors. Weight from saying "yes" a little too often.

And here was my husband explaining to me that if our plants get too much stress, they can't bear any fruit at all. I felt like the good Lord Himself were speaking to me at this pruning work session. *Cut, child, cut.*

Cutting can be hard, can't it? However, we must trust that pruning is biblical.

In John 15:1-2 we read Christ's own words: "I am the true vine, and my Father is the vinedresser. Every branch in me that does not bear fruit he takes away, and every branch that does bear fruit he prunes, that it may bear more fruit." Jesus wasn't talking about brambles of raspberries or blackberries; He was talking about the kingdom of God.

Straight from the mouth of Jesus, we learn that God is the true gardener. The vinedresser. The master planter. Jesus, the seed of God, is the true vine—the main vine. And we are called the branches of the vine (John 15:5). We spring forth as new growth from the true vine. Life can't occur without being attached to the vine.

This passage in John also tells us that God takes care of the vine and increases its fruitfulness by pruning branches that don't bear fruit. It's a beautiful but scary thought, right? I for one don't want to be cut off from the vine. So how can we branches stay healthy and away from those godly pruning shears? We follow the command to abide in Him (John 15:4).

This means we have to stay close to Jesus. Through prayer. Fellowship. Worship. Talking to Him, whether we are in the car or in church. When we abide in Jesus, our God is glorified, and we blossom as His disciples (John 15:7-8). We get to bear spiritual fruit for our ultimate gardener—fruit of love, joy, peace, patience, kindness, goodness, faithfulness, gentleness, and self-control (Galatians 5:22-23). Thus, spreading love and the truth to others.

Does it amaze you as much as it amazes me to see the truth of the gospel displayed in our natural world? Yes, I love sunset evenings such as this when my family is out tending to our vines. For me it's a period of reflection. Where I see the order of the universe coming full circle. Where I spend time quietly conversing with God about what I need to cut out of my life to make room for fruitfulness. It's a time to labor for my spiritual growth—as well as the sweet promise of a blackberry cobbler (with ice cream, of course!). Yes, even pruning is holy.

PRUNING CHALLENGE

Look at your calendar and obligations. What needs pruning from your life? Give yourself permission to grow by cutting. Society often tells us that more is better; however, God tells us that we have to cut back to grow. In other words, we must *let go to live*. This can be challenging.

One year, after much prayer and worry, I put aside my position as Vacation Bible School director at our church. When I stepped down from the position, I had no idea this book (or a new baby!) was on the horizon. But God did. I'm grateful I followed His leading. If I'd held on to being VBS director out of pride, I would have been smothered under the weight of pregnancy, family caretaking, and writing a book. I also would have stood in the way of allowing someone else the opportunity to bloom in that role.

God nudged me to prune my life.

Farm gal, it's not always the bad we need to cut from our lives, but also some of the good. We are called to bear fruit, so we must take care of our souls. John 15:8 says, "By this my Father is glorified, that you bear much fruit and so prove to be my disciples." Let's do the work of pruning so we can follow that direction.

Heavenly Father, help me identify the branches in my life that need pruning and give me the courage to make that clip. Amen.

MARCH

Trucks on the Farm

In his hand is the life of every living thing
and the breath of all mankind.

JOB 12:10

We have a fleet of old, beat-up trucks on our farm—from '80s-model pickups to one-ton flatbeds. We've got an old Ram or two, an antiquated Chevy or three, a Ford that needs to be retired, and several Toyotas past their prime but still trucking along. The collective worth of all these trucks probably equals one brand-new one. But when it comes to our trucks, we prefer antique (a nice way of saying "old"). Why get something new when it's just going to get dented and banged up in the fields?

These trucks haul feed, tow trailer-loads of cattle, and serve as a place for stargazing with the kids. These trucks are often dusty. And their tires are always muddy. But they are practical and work perfectly for us and our farmhands. And when they don't work perfectly, Perry, Robert, and Jackie fix them right up.

On occasion my husband drives over to the neighboring town for lunch meetings. Before leaving, he makes certain to exchange his muddy boots for a cleaner pair. Takes off his dirty coveralls. Even so, he often drives an old beat-up truck instead of one of our "newer" vehicles.

One day I climbed into the old flatbed truck and sat shotgun on the way to a restaurant with Perry. The dining establishment was bustling with the lunch crowd when we got there. I suppose it was the loud *boom, boom* of the engine that alerted patrons to our arrival. A dozen or so people standing outside turned and looked at us as we pulled into a parking spot.

I met the eyes of several in the group and watched as they turned up their noses with a *you don't belong here* expression on their faces. Which was humorous because it's not like we were at a fancy five-star restaurant.

Perry saw their reactions too. He laughed and said, "You finally see what I've been telling you for years. People think they are better than me when I drive one of our old trucks." He then quipped, "That's why I like driving 'em. Makes me instantly see the character of a person. Let's go eat."

Have you ever been judged for something you've worn or driven? Doesn't feel too great, does it? When we are judged, we often feel as if we are less than someone else.

Now let's turn this around. Have you ever made a value judgment of a person based on an outward attribute? Looked down on them for some reason or another?

Shamefully, I can raise my hand too. It's fleshly and sinful, and we've all done it. I remember sitting in an airport across from several affluent millennials who were obviously business colleagues, decked out in expensive clothing. I caught myself looking down on them, thinking they probably weren't nice folks. But how was I to know? They could have been the best people ever, but I judged them based on their perfectly tailored suits and designer luggage.

I judged the airline travelers based on outside appearances in the exact same way I was judged for stepping out of a dusty truck.

Judging is not justified in the eyes of the Lord. All our lives are of value. Why? Because God made us all. Job 12:10 says, "In his hand is the life of every living thing and the breath of all mankind." Pretty humbling! God created every one of us—those who wear Carhartt and those who wear Chanel. We should aim to see someone as a *child of God* first.

Once I walked hand in hand with a lady through the doors of our church. She was shaking, nervous because she thought she wouldn't be accepted at our country church with her tattoos and jeans. Her impression was that Christians always dressed up on Sundays (wrong!), and none of them have ink (also wrong!). Thankfully, when she walked into our sanctuary she was treated like royalty. It was almost like God had whispered to the women of our church, *Make her feel loved and welcome.* Ladies wearing dresses and ladies wearing jeans loved on this new gal. She was viewed as a fellow child of God. She felt welcomed and soon discovered lots of tattooed people sit in the rows of our church—including my husband.

Farm gal, let's commit to making people feel welcome. We are all God's handiwork. Whether you see someone driving a dusty pickup or a Mercedes, don't look down upon them or turn up your nose; see them as a fellow creation of God's. And whenever you feel as if you are being looked down upon, remember that God tells us we all belong.

MIND YOUR MANNERS

A smile and a pleasant word are the surefire way to greet someone kindly. Commit to treating everyone that way. We are all made in the image of God. All it takes is a "Nice to see you," a smile, or a head tilt and grin.

Of course, another way to show kindness is with a sweet treat!

When you need to bring dessert to a church social or other type of gathering, this is the ticket. This strawberry pretzel salad recipe is a crowd-pleaser from my friend Tonya. It's also a good reason to freeze fresh strawberries in the spring to keep year-round in the freezer (but berries from the store work just fine too).

Tonya's Strawberry Pretzel Salad

Crust

- 2⅔ cup crushed pretzels
- 2 tsp. sugar
- ¾ cup (1½ sticks) butter, melted

Cream cheese layer

- 1 pkg. (8 oz.) softened cream cheese
- 1 cup sugar
- 1 container (8 oz.) whipped topping

Strawberry layer

- 2 cups boiling water
- 1 package (6 oz.) strawberry gelatin
- 4 cups fresh strawberries (or 32 oz. frozen strawberries)

Preheat oven to 375°. Mix the crust ingredients together and press into a 9 x 13-inch pan. Bake for 10 minutes. Mix the cream cheese layer ingredients together and spread over the cooled pretzel crust. Bring water to a boil and pour it into the gelatin powder. Add strawberries. Allow the gelatin time to partially set. Then spread the strawberry mixture over the cream cheese layer. Chill for an hour. Enjoy!

⸎ MARCH ⸎

Seeds on the Farm

God so loved the world, that he gave his only Son, that whoever believes in him should not perish but have eternal life.

JOHN 3:16

Seeds. They're smooth and come in all different shapes and sizes. We grasp a packet of them, carefully chosen by the variety, and have a mindset of glorious expectation.

Manifold increase.

In your imagination, take a seed packet, pour the contents into the palm of your hand, and gaze at the handful of husks. Run your fingers across the hulls. These seeds are worthy—not necessarily for their present state (although many of us do enjoy eating sunflower and pumpkin seeds), but for the future.

These individual seed casings hold life inside them. They are capsules of life just waiting to be placed into the soil, where they will sit for a bit of time and then grow into a new form.

A creation anew.

Remember that field I love to gaze at while sitting at my farmhouse table? Right now, seeds are going into it. The temperature is just right—not too cold. The ground is just right—not too wet, and not too hard. The weather has been monitored, and conditions have been judged to be just right. The farmer knows the sun is gifting glorious spring rays to the land for just enough hours each day to warm the soil, so that come June we will have a crop of sweet corn.

One of the farm guys is out on that old red Massey Ferguson, pulling a Ford two-row mechanical corn planter, planting seeds right into the rows of tilled soil.

Drop. Drop. Drop.

The seeds drop into the earth, one at a time. The blade on the corn planter opens the ground, creating a notch just big enough for a solitary seed to be buried into the ground, and the drive wheel covers the seed with a blanket of dirt. Deep in the ground. Away from the sunshine. Nestled in the darkness.

Into the dark.

But soon into the light.

The seed will be altered from its original form. Leaving behind its old self in the ground. Emerging afresh.

The life within each seed spends much time just waiting, patiently, for soil with the right temperature and the right level of moisture to awaken it from its slumber.

The seed begins to swell as it absorbs the moisture surrounding the casing. Then, what is inside that casing begins the process of growth.

The process of germination. We learned about it in school, right? The life form inside that casing divides. The roots burrow deep into the soil and the sprout rises, rises, rises until it bursts through the soil. That tiny sprout will eventually become a stalk of corn—housing multiple ears. Ready to be eaten. The solitary multiplied.

Perfectly amazing, right? How the seed goes into the dark ground, where the old self is left behind—ceasing to be—so new life can rise. Rise to bear fruit. Rise to prosper.

Are you feeling a parallel yet? To our spiritual selves. And to the very foundation of our Christianity: the crucifixion, the burial, the rising.

As Easter draws near, the time when we celebrate the resurrection of Jesus, let's reflect on the miraculous act God ordained—and the miraculous sacrifice Jesus made so each and every one of us can have new life.

> If anyone is in Christ, he is a new creation. The old has passed away; behold, the new has come (2 Corinthians 5:17).

Christ's death and resurrection took place at a time ordained by God. The time was just right according to our Maker. And we celebrate His death and resurrection in the spring, the time of year when we reflect on the death of the old so the new can thrive.

It all does seem a bit strange and counterintuitive—death and then life? Even in farm talk it sounds mystical. Imagine an unknowing person watching the farmer plant seeds into the darkness of the ground. It would seem to be a hopeless situation to an observer unlearned in scientific ways. Why would something be buried in order to be born again? Why would we anticipate life from death?

And yet...God. The story of Easter. The ultimate death-to-life story.

Following the crucifixion of Jesus, Joseph of Arimathea took the bloodstained body—now seemingly just the hull of a man—and wrapped it in a clean linen cloth. He placed the body of Jesus into the darkness of a tomb. A tomb cut into the side of a rock, with a boulder covering the entrance (see Matthew 27:57-60).

Jesus laid to rest in total darkness.

Final. Story over. It seemed Jesus would stay in that darkness for eternity.

But on the third day, early in the morning, Mary Magdalene, along with others, went to the tomb where Jesus was buried. Expecting nothing more than death—but finding life.

An angel of the Lord appeared and said, "Do not be afraid, for I know that you seek Jesus who was crucified. He is not here, for he has risen, as he said. Come, see the place where he lay" (Matthew 28:5-6).

From the darkness He *arose*, bringing to us the most beautiful, bountiful blessing of all—eternal life. He died so our sins could be forgiven. And He rose so life could continue.

Farm gal, when we surrender ourselves to Christ, our God delights us with the expectation of what our growth can do to magnify His kingdom.

On our farm, when those seeds are dropped into the soil, we have expectations for growth. For increase. For harvest. And our seeds do, most often, bring forth life. But it is the mighty and true farmer—God—who arranged for His Son, Jesus, to be buried so that the most glorious increase of all could emerge: everlasting life.

For us. For our future generations.

Manifold increase.

Thank You, Father, for so loving the world that You gave us Your only Son—so that all of us who believe will not perish but have everlasting life with You. I pray that as I scoop up seeds this spring and place them into the earth, I will be reminded of the holiness and magnificence symbolized in this simple yet groundbreaking act. And may I be reminded each day that I must die to self in order to live in Christ. Amen.

GUSSIED UP

It's fun to dye Easter eggs and get them gussied up! However, I'm a failure when it comes to boiling eggs. I always have to look up directions. But my friend Amber is a master. This is her recipe for hard-boiling eggs (so you can dye them for Easter)—and then taking it a step further to make deviled eggs for Easter dinner. Amber is not one for exact measurements. She says, "Just keep adding until it looks right!"

Amber's Deviled Eggs

A dozen (or more) fresh eggs
1 tsp. baking soda
Mayonnaise
Spicy mustard
Sweet pickle relish
Salt
Pepper

Place eggs in cool water in a pot. Place pot on high heat. Add baking soda to the water. Bring to a boil and let boil for 10 to 12 minutes. Remove the eggs from the pot and rinse them with cold water for 2 to 3 minutes. Peel the eggs. Slice each in half and remove the yolk. Mash the yolk with mayonnaise, spicy mustard, and sweet pickle relish. Salt and pepper to taste. Now scoop a portion of the yolk mixture back into each divided egg. Enjoy!

APRIL

Puddles on the Farm

Rejoice in the Lord always; again I will say, rejoice.

PHILIPPIANS 4:4

An old wives' tale asserts that cows lie down in the pasture before a storm. This hasn't been scientifically proven (and the *Farmers' Almanac* actually calls it straight up "folklore"[1]), but I firmly believe the cattle on our farm are in touch with nature. Without consulting a weather app, they all seem to huddle and hunker down on the pasture when the winds start to change.

We can check a gazillion different weather sources to find out if a storm might be approaching our neighborhood. We usually know when it's time to take cover. In our modern society, the ferocity of the storm might catch us by surprise, but the fact that it is coming is usually a known variable.

However, when it comes to downpours of gloom, we have little warning that dark clouds might be coming our way.

Wouldn't it be nice to know when a figurative storm is about to approach our lives? Then we could just lie down and ready ourselves, like the cows in my pasture do—or maybe even jump the fence and run for the woods. But we can't always predict a spiritual, medical, or emotional storm—not the ferocity nor the timing. We just have to hunker down and face the circumstances.

Still, we are commanded to rejoice always. Philippians 4:4 says, "Rejoice in the Lord always; again I will say, rejoice." This is a pleasant command, but it can be difficult to follow. Who wants to rejoice when things aren't all sunshine and roses?

My kids, that's who.

Children have this uncanny ability to smile, rejoice, and find good in spite of and in the midst of unpleasant situations.

The remnants of storms often puddle our yard and driveway. These rainwater pools are brown and murky—far from rose colored, and they don't remind me of sunshine. The rain also causes the water levels to rise all over the farm. Our pond often overflows in the wake of a very heavy downpour, and so the grassland surrounding it becomes oozy and squishy.

It looks unappealing to me, but it's absolutely tantalizing to my children. One afternoon, when the skies cleared after a storm, I took my children to the perimeter of our front-pasture pond. It was a swamp all around. They begged to jump off our Ranger "just to look around," but pretty soon they were leaping, rolling, and sliding in mud.

I viewed the scene as a yucky pit. But my children viewed it as a free ticket to a water park. Or mud-wrestling pit. With big grins my kids splashed and splashed and splashed. Soon they were covered in the muck.

After resigning myself to the fact that the laundry would need a bit more scrubbing and the kids would need to be hosed off before entering our farmhouse, I came to see every splash as a holy reminder for me to rejoice. To savor the beauty of the moment.

The splashing became a catechism.

They would *splash*, and I would purposefully position my heart to *rejoice*.

Splash. Rejoice.

Splash. Rejoice.

Splash. Rejoice.

Yes, there are thunderstorms in life, but in every situation, we can find joy. We don't have to love the storm, but we can find glimmers of hope inside the storm.

When we look at the apostle Paul's command to rejoice, which was written while he was imprisoned, we learn we are to "rejoice in the Lord." We aren't told to rejoice in our circumstances, but to rejoice in the Lord.

How?

In his book *The Gospel of John*, Ronald Wallace writes, "Joy comes without being cultivated or thought about, to those who allow themselves to become absorbed, as John did, in the glory and wonder of...the Christ."[2] *Absorbed.* When we are absorbed in something, all other matters seem of secondary importance. My kids were absorbed in playing in the mud and didn't notice anything other than the fun.

Have you ever absorbed yourself in Christ and felt a sense of peace wash over your soul? C.S. Lewis wrote, "No soul that seriously and constantly desires joy will ever miss it. Those who seek find. To those who knock it is opened."[3] Can't we all, no matter our circumstances, reflect on the hope, promise, wonder, and truth of Christ when it is Him whom we seek? Our joy is not separate from Him but is *found* in Him. Confidence in the Lord is our joy.

As I watched my trio jump in those muddy puddles, with the cows standing and grazing nearby (no longer lying in the pasture), the geese calmly sitting on the pond, and llamas watching the scene, I knew that no matter the storm, no matter the weather, I could always choose joy by absorbing myself in the wonder of Christ.

For me the wonder was in the smiles upon their faces, the providence that the storm didn't last forever, and the earthly joys of the water, soil, and sky all meeting on the canvas of the farm horizon right before my eyes.

Let's rejoice *in* the Lord. The one who is our Creator, our provider, our strength, and our peace.

COME RAIN OR SHINE

Put on the rain boots of childlike enthusiasm and jump into *joy*. However your day is going, farm gal, go dance in the kitchen, take an outdoor walk, look through a seed catalog and imagine what you might plant, or grab a third or fourth cup of coffee, and then rejoice in the day that the Lord has made. Rejoice in Him.

This is the day that the LORD has made;
let us rejoice and be glad in it.

PSALM 118:24

APRIL

Goats on the Farm

No temptation has overtaken you that is not common to man. God is faithful, and he will not let you be tempted beyond your ability, but with the temptation he will also provide the way of escape, that you may be able to endure it.

1 CORINTHIANS 10:13

We made it almost two months with our trio of goats, but today they were loaded into the back of a black pickup and hauled away.

I consider myself a farm girl in the sense that I'm married to a full-time farmer. He's a tractor-driving, coveralls-wearing, salt-of-the-earth type of man. I like to ride around with him and enjoy the scenery. I'm not opposed to hard work or getting muddy, but I've learned that I draw the line when it comes to goat manure. I'm obviously not a full-fledged rural goddess. Yep. That's what my two-month stint as the proud owner of three goats taught me.

A kind neighbor man down the road gifted us the first two goats. And we acquired the third goat—a one-eyed beauty I named Gypsy—after another neighbor learned we were running a goat sanctuary. We own a rather large farm, but I was determined that the goats should take up residence in our backyard.

"The kids would love it!" I exclaimed.

"They'd mow the grass with their teeth!" I coaxed.

My husband tried talking me out of the endeavor. But I gave him a kiss and told him it would be just fine. So, yeah. It is my fault the goats became our backyard pets.

My husband built a fence. My kids helped name the goats. And we warmly welcomed Pickles, Brownie, and Gypsy to our backyard with a bucket of home-grown corn and a fresh bed of straw.

"Look, Perry. Our kids have their first pets!" I gushed after we brought them home.

The goats climbed to the top of the swing-set fort. They played in the water sprinklers with my kids. We fed them ice cream and peanut butter crackers. I bragged about them on Instagram. They were cute. And my kids loved them.

But you've probably heard a version of the saying, "Don't poop where you eat." Well, the goats evidently invented that phrase and made it their prime commandment for life. You see, we've got about an acre of lush grass and vegetation in our backyard. We have a very small concrete patio. Yep—the goats exclusively used the patio as their bathroom.

So every day I'd sweep and hose down the area. One day, while I was spraying the disaster, I realized I was wearing stilettos and cleaning up goat manure. Stilettos and manure don't go together.

The goats quickly became a little less bucolic in my mind. Then they started escaping their backyard sanctuary. It appears we had chosen a highly independent breed. People would come over for a visit and end up helping us chase goats around the yard. Our kids' babysitter even learned how to shepherd goats one night when she spied them out the window and feared they might not be able to swim. It's not that the grass was greener on the other side—it's that the concrete perimeter around the pool deck was calling their name.

Have I mentioned the goats would only poop on concrete?

I sent my husband a scathing text message. I told him that he didn't even need to try to fix the fence—we were finding a new home for those goats.

So we wrangled the goats and took them to our front pasture to live out the rest of their time with us in the company of our llamas. I told the kids we could still visit the goats, but if they stayed in the backyard we would never be able to swim in the pool. They had a choice. Turns out the pool trumped the goats.

Clearly, we have strong allegiances to our pets.

Unfortunately, the llamas and goats didn't coexist. It was a continual game of chase. I think the goats also realized that the pasture was a concrete-free zone.

So they escaped. And strolled into my front yard. We have a stamped-concrete porch. You get the drift.

Well, the goats almost lasted two whole months on the farm, but this morning Pickles, Brownie, and Gypsy were locked in a cage and placed under the custody of the county sheriff. The sheriff had heard about their plight. He says he came to rescue them. I say he came to arrest them for vandalism.

Whatever the case, the sheriff is a real-deal goat farmer. As for me…I've given up that title. I'm a farm gal—but I do have limits.

I KID YOU NOT

I hung on to those goats longer than I should have because of pride. I didn't want my husband to say, "Told you so!" Have you ever hung on to something too long, even though you knew it was messing up your life? Maybe you are hanging on to a bad habit. Or perhaps you are hanging on to a feud or disagreement, and you just can't bring yourself to say the apology.

It's tempting to hold on to things that cause us to sin. I can promise you the thoughts I was thinking about those goats were not holy—but I kept them longer than I should have. The Bible states, "No temptation has overtaken you that is not common to man. God is faithful, and he will not let you be tempted beyond your ability, but with the temptation he will also provide the way of escape, that you may be able to endure it" (1 Corinthians 10:13). I finally put pride aside and admitted that having concrete-going goats in the backyard wasn't a good idea. And I moved them to a farm where they would be loved and respected.

Perhaps you don't have goats in your backyard, but you might be holding on to something else because of pride.

Will you release it?

Pray to God. He is faithful. He always provides us a way to end these self-inflicted trials.

APRIL

Bees on the Farm

Fill your minds with those things that are good and that deserve praise: things that are true, noble, right, pure, lovely, and honorable. Put into practice what you learned and received from me, both from my words and from my actions. And the God who gives us peace will be with you.

PHILIPPIANS 4:8-9 GNT

Honey, *butter*, and *biscuit*.

Those three words sum up the absolute perfection of the Sunday dinners I used to enjoy at my grandmother Faye's house. I'd always skip the homemade strawberry preserves; I wanted my biscuits smothered with butter and drizzled with the nectar of the bees.

Domestic and wild bees live on our farm. A few years back we decided to purposefully make homesteads for bees. Terry, a church friend and neighbor, has been taking care of the colonies on our farm and trying to teach my husband the craft of beekeeping. We do it for the conservation and the pollination, but the honey is sure a nice by-product of our relationship with the honeybees!

Honey is harvested from the hives in summer. But right now, at the peak of springtime, the bees are busy. The queen sits in the hive and produces offspring, the drones serve the hive by mating with the queen (and then promptly dying!), while the worker bees perform a gazillion different jobs, including building honeycomb, guarding the hive, and being nurses for the young honeybees.

Of course, many of the bees have tasks related to the manufacturing of honey. And it's the honey we all love!

Forager bees are worker bees that fly out from the hives (up to three miles!) and take in the nectar from whatever nearby plants they find in bloom. Although I've never followed a bee on her mission, I've read that a worker bee can visit up to 1,000 flowers per day.

The taste, aroma, color, and texture of the honey we devour is all dependent upon what the worker bees take in when they are out foraging. For example, there are colonies of honeybees on the Big Island of Hawaii that only gather nectar from macadamia nut orchards for part of the year. When those orchards are in bloom, the bees are released so they can get to work! The much-coveted honey harvested from those tropical hives boasts a unique macadamia taste and dark coloring.[1]

Hawaii isn't the only state with special honey. Tupelo honey, made famous by songs and taste alike, is the result of bees being released into the swamps of Florida's Apalachicola region. The worker bees fly from their hives and take in the nectar from tupelo gum trees. Then they return to their bee homes to produce the luscious variety of honey that tantalizes many a taste bud.

Our bees can't boast that they live in a coastal state, but they do experience a pretty vibrant diet here on the farm. Our honeybees find nectar from apple tree blossoms, clovers, dandelions, goldenrods, sunflowers, blackberry blossoms, and lavender to take back to their hives. The honey we gather from their hives has more of a flavor-of-all Southern plants.

I used to think honey was honey. So I've been fascinated to learn that the taste is completely dependent upon what the worker bees harvest. Input influences output. Farm gal, we are like these bees; we put out what we take in.

Have you ever noticed how what you bring into your mind and soul eventually seeps out? Too much of the world placed into our souls, and we can become cranky, jealous, and irritable. Too much foul-mouthed music, and we can become foul mouthed. Too much listening to gossip, and we can become gossipy. Too much browsing social media, and we can become jealous.

But when we follow the clear instructions of the Bible, we tend to ooze a sweeter version of ourselves. Philippians 4:8-9 tells us, "Brothers, whatever is true, whatever is honorable, whatever is just, whatever is pure, whatever is lovely, whatever is commendable, if there is any excellence, if there is anything worthy of praise, think about these things. What you have learned and received and heard and seen in me—practice these things, and the God of peace will be with you."

Just like honeybees forage for lavender and clover blossoms, we should be foraging for blossoms that are true, honorable, just, pure, lovely, and commendable. Then it will be easier to live out those traits in our daily lives.

The Bible tells us what we should be foraging for and bringing into our hearts. And if we want to ooze sweetness and Christlike behavior, we best be putting those good things into our personal hives.

Now, excuse me while I go find a biscuit, butter, and some honey. I've made myself hungry!

SWEET AS HONEY

Honey tastes delightful on a biscuit, but have you ever tried it on a steak? Honey is a great ingredient in a marinade. Mix up this marinade and let it soak on your favorite cut of steak. We find that letting the steaks soak overnight makes them the most flavorful. Double or halve this recipe depending on how many folks you are feeding. Feel free to mess around with the ingredients as well. Some prefer more garlic than others. For a bit of zest, consider squeezing in some lime juice.

Honey Steak Marinade

- 1 cup honey
- 1 cup soy sauce
- 4 T. red wine vinegar
- 2 cloves garlic, crushed
- 2 T. freshly grated ginger
- ½ cup olive oil
- 4 steaks

Whisk the first six ingredients together. Put your steaks in a sealable bag and pour marinade into the bag. Place the bag in the fridge for at least an hour (although overnight works best). Take steaks out and grill. Enjoy!

❖ APRIL ❖

Deep Roots on the Farm

> I pray that you, being rooted and established in love, may have power...to grasp how wide and long and high and deep is the love of Christ.
>
> EPHESIANS 3:17-18 NIV

Both science and gardening 101 tell us that if you get a zinnia plant at your local gardening center and take it home, you can't just plop it out of its package, place it on *top* of the ground, and expect the plant to prosper.

Why? Because roots need to be *under* the soil. They must be away from the burning sunshine and within the safety of the nutrient-rich soil. Roots hold up the plant and transport nutrients and water to the rest of the plant. The root system, hidden deep underground, is the key ingredient of life for a stunner like a zinnia.

Yes, that is a basic gardening principle—you must plant the roots of a zinnia *in* soil.

Much to the chagrin of my farmer husband, I don't always follow basic scientific principles. I sometimes get distracted—which leads, I admit, to some shoddy work on my part. You could even say at times I'm a lazy planter.

Has that ever happened to you with a gardening project? A little *wishing for the best*?

You purchase something pretty from the local gardening center. You have grand plans to get the beauty in the ground and watch it bloom. You get your hands into the earth. Start digging. But the ground is hard, and it takes too much time to break through the soil. Then you get interrupted by a phone call or an unexpected visitor, or you can't find the shovel, or a child gets into mischief. So you hastily set the plant in the tiny hole you were able to create, sweep a little soil over the roots, and scoot away, crossing your fingers that you did a good-enough job.

The next morning, coffee in hand, you stroll out to admire your freshly planted flower garden. Except you spy a dead plant or two or three—or all of them. The stems stooped over…the blooms dried and discolored. You remember you forgot to water them. The roots weren't planted deep enough into the soil. The sun scorched those exposed roots. And scorched roots can't take water and nutrients to the rest of plant (especially if those roots are too shallow, and you forgot to give the plant a little love from the water hose).

Unfortunately, this has happened a time or two at my house.

You might be a master gardener and are in tears at my wayward ways. I promise…I'm learning. I'll try to do better this spring at rooting my plants deep in the soil and not bypassing this vital step. The roots of my zinnias (and all those plants I buy) should be planted deep, just like the roots of our faith must dwell deep in the love of Jesus.

ROOTED IN LOVE

I love what the apostle Paul writes to the church in Ephesus:

> I pray that out of his glorious riches he may strengthen you with power through his Spirit in your inner being, so that Christ may dwell in your hearts through faith. And I pray that you, being rooted and established in love, may have power, together with all the Lord's holy people, to grasp how wide and long and high and deep is the love of Christ, and to know this love that surpasses knowledge—that you may be filled to the measure of all the fullness of God (Ephesians 3:16-19 NIV).

This is one of my favorite images in the Bible—"being rooted…in love." Paul prays that Christ's followers will be rooted in the love of Christ. Healthy roots, as we recall from my zinnia mishap, are vital for life. Roots give strength (by transporting nutrients). Roots anchor the plant. Roots refresh the plant (with water).

In this scriptural imagery from Paul we see that we must be planted in the soil of *love*. The love of Christ gives us strength. The love of Christ is our anchor, holding us up through a variety of circumstances—when the sun beats, and when the rain pours. And the love of Christ refreshes us.

Our very foundation is love. Our strength and life are love. This comes from the love we receive from Christ and the love we give Christ.

As believers, we must stay rooted in this most important commandment. In Matthew 22:37-40 we read the words of Jesus: "You shall love the Lord your God with all your heart and with all your soul and with all your mind. This is the great and first commandment. And a second is like it: You shall love your neighbor as yourself. On these two commandments depend all the Law and the Prophets."

Farm gal, we need not worry that our spirits will wither or our blooms drop—as long as we stay rooted in the love of Christ. We can take care of our hearts by making sure our roots are planted deep in Him.

Heavenly Father, today I pray that I will dwell in You. I don't want a surface relationship with You. I know that's not life giving. I want to plant my roots by digging deep into my faith and growing my love and trust in You. Amen.

WEEDING

I learned from my grandfather that the best time to weed or hoe is in the early morning. It's cooler then. This makes the work more comfortable, plus the dampness of the early morning dew allows the roots to be pulled out of the ground more easily. Early morning weeding also helps eradicate the weeds because the exposed root that you've pulled from the ground gets scorched all day by the sun as it sits in the garden row.

Also, know your plants. I've known folks who have hoed rows of what they thought was the weed johnsongrass, only it was actually sprouts of corn shooting up from the garden. They hoed their crop and left the weeds growing.

MAY

Making Hay on the Farm

He who gathers in summer is a prudent son,
but he who sleeps in harvest is a son who brings shame.

PROVERBS 10:5

Do you know the difference between hay and straw? I have trouble telling them apart, and I constantly call bales the wrong name. My husband corrects me a million times over; the ag vocab just doesn't seem to stick in my head. However, one thing I do know with absolute certainty is that the phrase "Make hay while the sun shines" is a farm rule.

On our farm we do two cuttings of hay. Hay is what feeds our cattle. You've got to mow it and let it dry. Rake it into a windrow. Bale it into a round or square bale. Finally, transport it to where it can be stored. Then, throughout the fall and winter, the hay is delivered to the cattle for a healthy meal.

Our first hay is cut at the beginning of April, and we work straight through the month of June. Then we start all over come August. We cut hay on our own farm, on farms we lease, and for neighbors as well. Hay is one of our main crops—we need it to feed our cattle. Hay time is certainly one of the busiest seasons of our farm year (and it's a season that comes twice a year!). It ain't nothing to see a tractor going from the time the dew dries until the moon is high in the night sky. And big trucks and trailers haul hay to our barns for hours and hours and hours on end.

I should note that I'm using the word *we* very loosely here. I offer moral support. I keep the house running. I do a ton of activities—taking food to the field and holding down the fort at our home—but I don't drive a tractor or lift square bales. The *we* I'm talking about is my husband and the team of amazing folks who work on our farm. I salute all those farmhands who come early and stay late.

The work is constant. But the one thing that brings hay production to a standstill is rain. Haymaking is completely dependent on the weather. When the hay is ready and the sun is shining, the tractors take to the fields. When it's raining, other work is accomplished, haymaking is abandoned for the day, and prayers go up to the good Lord to make the sun shine soon.

This is where the saying "Make hay while the sun shines" comes from. The phrase, likely originating in medieval Europe, was not created because farmers are afraid of getting wet. We all know farmers work through rain, sleet, snow, and drought. Rather, the phrase speaks to the truth that a farmer must work hard when the conditions are right. Wet hay is a disaster and completely worthless. Farmers have to take advantage of the sun-kissed opportunities or lose their shot. Weather is monitored and plans are made to work around the clock when the elements are favorable. My husband (and many of our farm workers) don't get to *hit the hay* until well after midnight during haymaking season.

WHILE THE SUN SHINES

God provides all of us those seasons when the sun shines a bit brighter. He gives us opportunities, and all signs point toward *go*. Time to get to the field and do the work!

As a mama I have short periods of time when I can get about my business of writing. My husband can't bale hay when it is raining, and I can't write when my foursome are all underfoot. Nope, I have to make my proverbial hay when the kids are napping, when I can get a grandmother to babysit, or in the wee hours of the morning or night. If I don't take advantage of those times, then the book will not get written. Likewise, if my husband doesn't lead the crew to work during the sunshine and moonshine, the hay will not get put up.

We all have obligations. All types of work. Farm gal, we must take advantage of the time God provides. We have to be—as Proverbs 10:5 says—"prudent" with our time. What does this mean? It means to discern our hours wisely. To our Lord it is disgraceful to sleep straight through the harvest period when He has provided a bounty for us to reap.

How can we be prudent with our time and not lazy? When the crop is in, we must focus on the tasks at hand, thank Him for the opportunity to bring in a harvest, put forth our very best effort, and work till completion. Yes, hitting the hay is important, but so is making hay!

As we go about making the hay in our own lives, let's position our hearts to praise God for the crop—and for making the conditions favorable for us to go about our God-provided work.

HAY AND STRAW

What is the difference between hay and straw?

Hay is grass like fescue, alfalfa, or timothy that is harvested while alive and then dried out. Usually the seed is left intact. Hay is used as feed for animals. It contains nutrients and is usually greenish in color.

Straw is the stalk remnant of a dried-out crop and is not usually fed to livestock. Wheat straw is an example. After the wheat is harvested, the stalks left behind are bundled to use as a ground cover, to mulch a garden, or to bed barnyard animals. It is a golden color.

How, exactly, does one "make hay"?

Make sure rain is not in the immediate forecast. Usually we follow a three-day schedule per field on our farm. But, of course, things change.

Following is a perfect-world schedule of making hay. We put up around five hundred acres of hay two or three times a year.

- **Day 1:** Cutting (or raking). We use a mower conditioner (disc mower) that is pulled behind a tractor. It mows the hay down. There are rollers or flails behind the cutter that crimp the hay. This allows the hay to dry out quicker. The hay is left in a line on the field where it was cut. It sits overnight to allow the hay to cure in the field.
- **Day 2:** Tedding. We use a hay tedder. This device, pulled behind a tractor, scatters and flips and fluffs the hay so the hay further cures out in the sunshine.
- **Day 3:** Raking and baling. We use a hay rake that is pulled behind a tractor. This rakes the hay into a neat windrow. Once the hay is in a windrow, then the hay is baled into a square or round bale. The hay is kept together with twine or netting. Once hay is baled, it will usually be taken to a hay barn for storage.

TIP: Wait until after the morning dew has dried before starting each step. My father, Dale, says that around here, if it is going to be 80 degrees or above, it's a great day to make hay.

MAY

Rambo on the Farm

Stay close to anything that makes you want to do right.
Have faith and love, and enjoy the companionship of
those who love the Lord and have pure hearts.

2 TIMOTHY 2:22 TLB

Rambo had a reputation for throwing some pretty lambs and also for throwing the legs out from under folks. For those of you who aren't farmers, this means he fathered great-looking offspring but was also downright mean.

He sauntered into our pasture solely for the purpose of procreation. Our ewes needed to mate, and he was the ram for the job. He also arrived with a stern warning from our rancher friend Andy (the ram's owner): "Don't let Sarah or them kids get in the pasture with him."

Perry advised me that Andy and his wife, Annette, had both been bucked and bruised by the ram we all affectionately called Rambo. It was obvious Rambo sauntered through life with an attitude. However, I didn't listen very well. I sometimes have a penchant for overlooking advice—even advice from those who love me.

Perry would try to get in the pasture to feed Rambo, and the ram would charge. We'd stand by the fence to try to pet the sheep, and he would charge. Basically, Rambo was now in charge of the front pasture.

I requested that he immediately be handed an eviction notice. My kids and I wanted to be able to pet the horse in the pasture and not have our sweet sheep bossed around by such a surly male. But my husband said that our sheep needed to be bred. He asked for me to be patient and told me *not to enter* the pasture.

Some time passed; I grew impatient. Rambo had completed his mission, yet he remained in our pasture.

"Get him out of here!" I'd often say.

"Andy don't want him back," my husband would remark.

That was that, and the ram remained.

Well, one day, when I was nine months pregnant, I loaded the two-year-old and the five-year-old in our doorless UTV and opened the gate to the pasture. We were going to ride to the pond and see our animals, and our UTV would be our tank to protect us from Rambo.

What could go wrong, right?

We stopped to see the baby lambs. Then the llamas and our horse came up to our little farm vehicle. They serenely crowded around. We petted them; I took pictures. Out of the corner of my eye I noticed that Rambo had joined the crowd.

But I felt invincible and went on oohing and aahing at the ewes.

Then suddenly Rambo charged at the Ranger, aiming his horns straight toward my nine-month-full belly that was wedged up to the steering wheel.

I slammed the accelerator to the floor and zoomed forward so Rambo would hit the tail end of the vehicle instead of my body. I narrowly missed Rambo charging into my womb.

My kids were shocked, alarmed, and all in a tizzy. They may have had a few bruises as well from being slammed against the dashboard.

We left the pasture.

A few weeks later I delivered our third child and noticed, after arriving home, that the ram was no longer with us. But his legacy lives on. My Sophie, who is not terrified of anything, will sprint as fast as she can toward safety if you even joke about a ram coming toward her.

Has an event like this ever happened in your life before? You are warned. You don't heed the warning. You face the consequences. I'm sure we all have several hundred instances of this formula playing out in our personal histories.

Pastor Russ, my preacher, recently gave a sermon on sin. We read in our Bibles about the Lord warning Cain: "If you do not do what is right, sin is crouching at your door; it desires to have you, but you must rule over it" (Genesis 4:7 NIV).

The Lord was warning Cain that sin would overtake him if he didn't make good choices and got too close to sin. Cain didn't heed the warning and ended up killing his brother Abel. Pastor Russ pointed out that sin is described as crouching at our door, just waiting for us to show weakness so we will entertain it. Then it pounces and brings us down.

Well, that immediately made me think of Rambo. I had been warned about the danger. I knew that the danger was severe and could bring me down. I thought I could get close to the danger without being affected.

I was wrong.

Rambo, just like sin, was waiting for me to open the gate and come close. Then that devil in a ram suit pounced. I'm lucky that Rambo didn't leave us with anything more than a few bruises and a healthy fear of rams.

But he did show me that we can't walk in pastures full of evil and not expect to be affected. The devil is mighty and looks for opportunities to attack our weak spots. The good Lord gives us this warning in the very first book of the Bible. Perhaps we should pay attention. We must stay aware of our surroundings and emotions and not unlock the gates of sin.

Farm gal, sin does desire to rule over us, but we have to use the wisdom from God to rule over these unholy desires. That means not stepping a foot into any pasture of temptation, but rather drawing close to goodness.

CLOSE THE GATE CHALLENGE

Read 2 Timothy 2:21-22 (TLB).

> If you stay away from sin you will be like one of these dishes made of purest gold—the very best in the house—so that Christ himself can use you for his highest purposes. Run from anything that gives you the evil thoughts that young men often have, but stay close to anything that makes you want to do right. Have faith and love, and enjoy the companionship of those who love the Lord and have pure hearts.

Don't you love that translation?

We have the choice to be a gold dish used by Christ. But to experience this highest honor we must run from temptations and stay close to what makes us want to do right—which includes staying close to "those who love the Lord and have pure hearts."

I want you to get out a piece of paper and a pen (or you can go wild and pull out some art supplies). Draw a big square on your paper. In the center, draw a cross. The square represents the pasture of your soul. The cross represents Christ.

Next, draw some little circles in the square. Think of these as your "livestock." Label them with the names of people, places, things, or ideas that make you want to do what is right.

Now sketch out a trailer. Draw some more circles of livestock on that trailer and label them as things that tempt you to sin. Imagine driving that trailer down the road and say, "Get outta here and don't come back!"

Study your drawing, then tuck it someplace safe. Keep coming back to it, and let it remind you to nurture those livestock that encourage you to dwell in Christ—and send away the livestock that tempt you to sin.

Lord, thank You for giving me the ultimate piece of advice—to stay away from sin. Please help me heed Your warnings. Amen.

MAY

Picnics on the Farm

He who plants and he who waters are one, and each will receive his wages according to his labor. For we are God's fellow workers. You are God's field, God's building.

1 CORINTHIANS 3:8-9

Farm-to-table dinners are the hottest tickets in town. But here on the farm we have *table-to-farm* dinners—meaning we take dinner to the field.

I must admit, these field dinners are not as gourmet as many of the six-course menus I've seen advertised at those farm-to-table epicurean events—which boast local and fresh cuisine specially prepared by a chef. Yes, most connoisseurs aren't going to appreciate the bologna and cheese sandwiches I bring to the pasture for my husband to enjoy. But Perry certainly loves them!

My family sits on the back of the truck or the hay wagon, or I set out a blanket for us to sit on in the middle of the pasture. The kids eat quickly and then run through the hayfield—often jumping atop the round bales. After we eat, Perry takes each of our kids along with him on the tractor for a few trips around the field, and then the kids and I head home so I can get them tucked in for the night.

I wasn't always so kind as to bring a tote of food to my husband in the field. Early in our marriage I was agitated that Perry rarely came home for dinner in the spring or summer. He works hard not only to provide for our family, but also to keep the farm going and to make sure our cattle have feed for the winter. But instead of looking at the big picture, I was miffed that the only time I saw my husband was if I hopped on the John Deere with him.

On the weekdays I'd often teach all day, go home, grade papers, prepare lessons, eat dinner by myself, and then tuck myself into bed. Weekends weren't any better; farming is not a 40-hour-week job. Loneliness was not how I had imagined married life.

The wicker picnic basket I'd purchased, with the romantic intent of dinner beneath the stars, just sat in the pantry gathering dust. Our date nights were few and far between and entirely dependent upon the weather. It's hard to make plans with a farmer.

Well, farm gal, I finally pulled up my big-girl britches and had a change of heart. Instead of sulking at home, I realized I could pack that picnic and go to my husband instead of sitting at home brooding that my notions of marriage weren't being realized.

Sometimes we've got to meet people where they are, don't we?

Yes, making hay while the sun shines means Perry spends most of his spring and early summer evenings in the field. But I no longer mope like I did early in our marriage, and Perry has made positive changes regarding how he spends his time as well. Now, during haymaking season, I often take dinner to the field so my kids and I can spend time with Perry, show him love, and revive him with cheer and food.

I'm not a farmer, but I am Perry's coworker. My job just looks a little different than his. Yet we are equally important. And we appreciate each other.

Our picnic dinners in the hayfield have come to symbolize the give and take of marriage. We've both grown as husband and wife by adjusting our outlook. Quarreling, sulking, and wishing for a different reality make for a pretty bad marriage.

Divisions in labor can be a sore spot for anyone. Not only within marriage and the family, but also within the fellowship of believers. Yep, arguing can lead to a desolate existence.

The apostle Paul wrote a letter to the Corinthian church addressing issues they were having—and one big issue was arguing over who was best. According to 1 Corinthians, the folks in the Corinthian church were arguing over which apostle of Christ they followed. Paul heard about this quarrel and tried to put a stop to it. He wrote them a letter and provided a nice farm analogy for the church to chew on.

Paul asked them to imagine a field. In this field one person does the planting. One person does the watering. "Who is more important?" he seemed to ask. "The planter or the waterer?"

Scratching your head? Paul settled the church squabble by saying, "God...gives the growth" (1 Corinthians 3:7). Paul pointed out that the one who plants and the one who waters are equal. "He who plants and he who waters are one, and each will receive his wages according to his labor. For we are God's fellow workers. You are God's field, God's building" (verses 8-9).

Paul was saying that no one laborer is more important than the next. Rather, the glory of *any type* of growth or creation goes to God; we are nothing without Him. It's futile and sinful for us to argue over who is the best among Christians. We are all important. Some of us plant. Some of us hoe. Some of us bring the bologna sandwiches. But to God we are equals. It is Him and only Him who should be revered.

Isn't it neat to know that we all bring something to the table, as the expression goes? The very table of our esteemed God! Through the words of Paul, God reminds us we are all appreciated in His kingdom. Whatever He has us bring to the table is worthy. Whether we are at home wrestling kids or out tedding hay or preaching to thousands, we are all equally important. You and I are called "God's fellow workers" (1 Corinthians 3:9).

Now, I challenge you to spread this love around and go show your appreciation to a fellow laborer in God's kingdom. Pack that picnic and meet them in whatever field they are toiling. Just try not to be like the Corinthians and pick a fight.

We've all got a choice: We can pack a punch, or we can pack a picnic. But which will advance the kingdom of God further?

The wicker basket for the win!

PACK A LUNCH

My mother-in-love, Ruthe, has packed plenty of farm picnics. Our favorite addition to the basket is her pimento cheese.

Ruthe's Pimento Cheese

- 1 jar pimentos (4 oz.) with juice
- 3–4 T. sugar
- 3/4 cup mayonnaise
- 2 lb. Velveeta cheese (or 1 lb. Velveeta and 1 lb. sharp cheddar), shredded

In a large bowl mix diced pimentos (with juice) and sugar. Then add mayonnaise (she prefers Miracle Whip). Mix well by hand and slowly add shredded cheese while continuing to mix. Add additional mayonnaise if you need it for consistency and salt and pepper to taste. Enjoy on crackers or spread between two slices of bread for a sandwich. This picnic-sized recipe easily makes enough for 18 to 24 sandwiches.

MAY

Bursting with Worship on the Farm

Let the fields and their crops burst out with joy!
Let the trees of the forest sing for joy.

PSALM 96:12 NLT

Most of the churches in our two-red-light town host an event each Sunday morning. It's an event called a worship service. Some also refer to this as "big church."

At our Baptist church we listen to the choir sing, join our fellow pew sitters in singing hymns, greet one another, take up an offering, study the Bible through a message shared by our preacher, and pray. It's a holy time where we commune with one another and our Lord.

(We often end this service with a time of "fellowship." Meaning we devour fried chicken, homemade rolls, mashed potatoes, and a gazillion desserts at a potluck luncheon.)

Worship, by definition, is showing adoration to our Lord. It's a matter of the heart. A time when we show our King we revere Him. We celebrate, exalt, respect, extol, magnify, and praise Him. (Yes, I consulted the thesaurus. Aren't those synonyms lovely?) Truly, worship is an outward expression of the internal joy we feel toward the Lord.

Worship can take place in the communal setting of a church service—but it can also come at any time throughout the day and take many different forms. In fact, because of the recommendation for social distancing that began in

2020, our church is currently having services via online streaming. We are on the couch, not in the pew. And God can be with us in either place, can't He?

We can also raise a hallelujah in the car or while washing dishes. Worship happens when we sing to God, talk to Him, read and memorize His Word, and show His love to His people. It can happen in a lot of other ways too. Worship is very personal, a matter of the heart. In a way, worship means bursting forth with joy because of our appreciation of Him.

Right now, I can sit on the front porch of my farmhouse and see all kinds of worshipers praising the Lord. The wildflowers are bursting forth with pinks, purples, and yellows. My roses are all shades of pink. The blackberry vines are a verdant green. The irises my father-in-law planted at the north end of my house are gifting us a rainbow to the eyes. I can smell the honeysuckle, view the maple tree full of life, and even spy a few dots of red strawberries coming up from the little patch nearby.

Think I'm crazy calling all these plants worshipers? Well, Psalm 96:12 (NLT) says, "Let the fields and their crops burst out with joy! Let the trees of the forest sing for joy." King David was describing the bursting beauty of the crops, fields, and plants as an act of worship at the coming of the Lord's kingdom. Here is the verse in context:

> Let the heavens be glad, and the earth rejoice!
> Let the sea and everything in it shout his praise!
> Let the fields and their crops burst out with joy!
> Let the trees of the forest sing for joy
> before the LORD, for he is coming!
> He is coming to judge the earth.
> He will judge the world with justice,
> and the nations with his truth (verses 11-13 NLT).

That'll preach!

Those roses and strawberries I see are certainly showing God worship with such vibrancy. And there truly is joy at the coming harvest for those of us who have Jesus in our hearts.

Some of us a get a bit fearful at the thought of the coming of the Lord. Opening the book of Revelation can cause our hands to shake. But in this passage from Psalm 96, David overwhelmingly reminds us that we should *feel* joy at the coming of the King and *showcase* this joy to Him.

As Christians we aren't going to spontaneously burst forth with edible fruit or vibrant colors—however, David tells us we can "sing to the Lord, bless his name"; we can "tell of his salvation" (Psalm 96:2); and we can "come into his courts" (verse 8) to "worship the Lord in the splendor of holiness" (verse 9).

Farm gal, the crops and trees have Sunday service right where they are when they are in season. When life is within them, they are found worshiping our Creator. We should do the same—inside and outside the church building.

Can I get an "amen"?

TASTE THE GOODNESS

Cobbler is queen around these parts. So simple. So yummy. In this cobbler recipe, you can substitute any fruit for the blackberries. You can also get fancy and combine fruits. Blackberry and peach cobbler is awfully tasty!

Tip: When using fresh fruit, mash the fruit a bit to release the juices. If there is still not enough juice, add a cup or so of warm water and some sugar to the bowl in which you are mashing the fruit.

Gretchen's Blackberry Cobbler

½ cup (1 stick) butter
2 cups self-rising flour
1½ cups sugar
1 cup buttermilk or whole milk
Splash of vanilla
4 cups fresh blackberries
Bit of sugar for topping

Preheat oven to 350°. Place butter in a 9 x 13-inch baking dish, then place the dish in the warm oven. While the butter melts, prepare the batter. To prepare the batter, sift the flour and sugar into a bowl. Add the buttermilk and vanilla. Beat well and pour into the baking dish of melted butter. *Do not* stir the butter and batter together. Spoon fruit with its juice evenly over the batter. Sprinkle sugar on top. Bake for about 45 minutes or until brown on top. Serve with ice cream. Enjoy!

SUMMER

WELCOME SUMMER

She smelled of sun and daisies with a hint of river water.

KATIE DAISY

Smell the fresh hay being made? See the watermelons? Hear the tractors rumbling? Summer is here, which means farm tasks are plenty, but opportunities for fun are all around too! Some of our summer tasks here on the farm include...

- mowing hay
- building fences
- checking on crops
- tilling garden soil and cropland
- harvesting honey and sweet corn
- tending the garden
- giving minerals to the cattle

Farm gal, this summer let us rejoice in the grandeur of God's creation. Let's spend some time this week scribbling out our summer intentions. Of course, just like on a farm, plans change. It's okay if our intentions don't all garner check marks. The best-laid plans often go awry, as the poet Robert Burns noted. Let's enjoy the ride!

What might you like to...

- *plant in your life?* What can you sow?
- *cultivate in your life?* What can you tend to that's already growing?
- *prune in your life?* What do you need to discard or trim a bit?

PICK A SCRIPTURE

What scripture can you meditate on for the summer season?

PRAY A PRAYER

Heavenly Father, may we gather all the goodness You have blooming for us this summer. Let us take time to make wildflower bouquets and jump in the river. We worship You by rejoicing in the grandeur of Your creation.

JUNE

Fireflies on the Farm

The heavens declare the glory of God,
and the sky above proclaims his handiwork.

PSALM 19:1

When was the last time you went outside at dusk and stayed out until nightfall, lingering in the open air? Has it been a while?

Henry James said, "Summer afternoon—summer afternoon; to me those have always been the two most beautiful words in the English language."[1] But I disagree with the novelist. *Summer evenings* are, without question, the most beautiful words in our language—at least in our Southern vernacular. Summer evenings are made for lingering. The stars. The warm breeze. The quiet.

For me, the official arrival of summer is when the fireflies start dancing through the pastures. I'm as giddy as can be when I see the first one light up the night. My children love to run through the yard chasing them. It's not unusual for us to remain outdoors way past the time the stars and moon take their positions.

Are childhood memories replaying through your mind right now? Recall evenings of nothingness that were everything: chasing the enchanting sparks, catching them, and then collecting them in Mason jars.

It was so carefree, wasn't it?

Lightning bugs—fireflies—are incarnate wonder, a tangible enchantment created by God. They beckon us to slow down. To simplify. To gaze. These nocturnal flying beetles, which are found on all but one continent, spend their mornings and afternoons lying low to the ground. But as night falls, they emerge from their slumber in the grass and begin their flights of love. Did you know they flash their lights as a mating "call"? The males flash. And when a female sees the firefly of her desire, she flashes in return. It's a dance. A glowing symphony—not for our ears, but for our eyes.

> The heavens declare the glory of God,
> and the sky above proclaims his handiwork (Psalm 19:1).

It is on these summer evenings, when lightning bugs twirl and pirouette through the air, that I feel we can fully revel in God's craftsmanship.

Farm gal, I know our lives can get busy. I know we have dishes to wash. We have children to tuck in and bedtime stories to read. Laundry to wash. Emails to answer. The news cycle to watch. The next day to plan. But as summer begins let's resolve not to *do more* but to *marvel more*. Let's resolve to stop and marvel at God's majesty.

The best place to start? Outdoors, of course. It is quite impossible to stand in the big black expanse of night with the cosmos above and the grass below and not praise Him. Spend five minutes—or an hour or several as the day makes its final adieu. Catch a firefly or two. Supply your children with Mason jars. Stare at the stars. Grab a blanket and lie in your backyard with your face toward the moonlight and the constellations. Resist the urge to reach for your phone. Don't communicate with friends on social media; instead, communicate with your Maker and those in the flesh right beside you.

COME SIT A SPELL

Henry David Thoreau wrote, "God himself culminates in the present moment, and will never be more divine in the lapse of all ages."[2] As we spend time this summer admiring the lightning bugs, let's marvel in the presence of the present—a gift to us from the Maker Himself.

Heavenly Father, I commit to marveling at Your workmanship.
I will gaze at the stars and watch the dance of the fireflies.
I will feel the night breeze as I sit in the quiet.
I will smell the honeysuckle vines. I will hear the frogs
croaking, the katydids performing their evening symphony,
and You whispering to me. Lord, this summer I shall
praise You by reveling in Your creation. Amen.

JUNE

Planting Pumpkins on the Farm

I am the true vine, and my Father is the gardener.

JOHN 15:1 NIV

Some folks get a tad bent out of shape when stores start bringing out Christmas decorations in July (or maybe it's now Saint Patrick's Day when Santa makes his yearly debut). It seems all the seasons tend to run together in the shopping aisles.

"It's too early to be thinking about the next holiday!" or "Let the turkey have his day!" we mutter to our friends. We treat the arrival of holiday supplies on store shelves as if Thanksgiving were a neglected child whose birthday gets passed over for that of a more favored sibling.

But here on the farm, we identify a bit with the "jumping to the next season" quandary of the stores. Because here it is, June 15—a day hotter than tarnation—and we are thinking about October. The farmer has us out in the freshly plowed soil planting pumpkins.

You see, whatever we hope to harvest in the fall must be planted months and months in advance. So, into the worked soil go the pumpkin seeds.

For us, the method of planting is very hands on—or should I say, "boots on"? The soil has been worked by the cutting harrow. But we plant our acre plot of pumpkins without using any machinery. We walk down a row, and my husband, using his boot-clad foot, sweeps the soil to create a little hill in the center of the row. Into this little raised area go the seeds. Planted not too deep—an inch will do just fine.

We continue this process—him sweeping little hills in the rows, and us dropping seeds into the mounds—until the seeds run out. All in all, we plant around three seeds per hill, with the hills about ten feet apart.

Over the next several months we will take care of the pumpkins. The kids and I will go up to the patch to check the progress. We will first see tiny sprouts emerge from where we planted the seeds. Then we will see those sprouts turn into sprawling vines. Vines will be all over the field! Offshoots from the main vine will take off in their own directions.

In a month or two we will see blossoms emerge on the vines, and from those blossoms small, green pumpkins will grow. But we must be patient and not pick too early. With time, the pumpkins will grow larger and larger until they reach maturity.

In the fall, we will start picking pumpkins from those vines that started out as these tiny seeds going into the ground on this hot June afternoon. And after we enjoy the pumpkins, we will gather some of the seeds, dry them out, and store them so we can plant them the following June.

Yes, I guess you could say we are always looking ahead. Not only to the next season, but also to the next year. The planting we are doing right now will ensure a pumpkin harvest legacy. Not only will we enjoy the pumpkins in the fall, but the heirloom seeds we save from those harvested pumpkins will be planted in the coming years, providing us a future filled with pumpkin crops.

This mindset of forward thinking is part of farming; however, we are leaving the fall decorating until fall actually arrives. No flannel-wearing scarecrows for us right now, even if we are spending the day planting pumpkins!

This hot work is made joyful by the knowledge that in just a few months we will be gathering our future jack-o'-lanterns and harvesting the main ingredient in pumpkin pie. But what's even more special is that some of the seeds we are planting today came from a package we'd forgotten we had in our possession. A few years ago my grandmother Faye had scraped the seeds out of a pumpkin we'd grown for her and saved them for us. She carefully wrote on the package the year and variety. We'd placed the seed packet in our freezer and were surprised to find it a few days ago. Today those seeds went in the ground.

SAVING HEIRLOOM SEEDS

Take the seeds out of pumpkins, butternut squash, tomatoes, watermelons, or whatever vegetable or fruit plant you wish to save. Rinse the seeds with plain water (don't use detergent). Immediately spread out the seeds on a newspaper, so each individual seed can dry out. This drying process might take a few days. Once the seeds are completely dry, fold them up in the newspaper they are lying upon and place the newspaper into a freezer bag (or in an airtight container). Seal the bag (or container) and label it with the variety and year. Place in the freezer until you wish to plant the seeds. Do allow the seeds to thaw at room temperature for 24 hours before planting. (This method works for heirloom seeds but not hybrid seeds. Hybrid plants are created from cross-pollination of two plant varieties. Seeds from these plants do not save well from year to year. Heirloom plants are grown from seeds that have been handed down for generations. These plants are also open pollinated, and the "traits" of the plant save well in seed form from year to year. We grow both types on our farm!)

Those seeds my grandmother Faye had saved a few years back are now having the chance to grow. To bloom. To bear fruit. The little seeds had lain dormant. But today they are being given the opportunity to sprout. My grandmother had invested her time so that future pumpkins would grow on our farm.

FOR FUTURE GENERATIONS

Just like the plants in our fields, we will all pass something down. In his book *East of Eden*, John Steinbeck wrote, "You're going to pass something down no matter what you do or if you do nothing. Even if you let yourself go fallow, the weeds will grow and the brambles. Something will grow."[1]

Yes, the work we do today can impact future generations. But our work for the Lord can create the most important legacy ever: the legacy of Christ. The legacy of eternity.

What are we passing down in our lives? Weeds or goodness?

⯌ JUNE ⯌

Heaven's Dew on the Farm

The vine shall give its fruit, and the ground shall give its produce, and the heavens shall give their dew.

ZECHARIAH 8:12

Outside, a flood was falling. Rain pelting. Thunder rolling.

Inside, safe within the church sanctuary, a roomful of kids was riled and wet from getting caught in the June downpour.

As the director of Vacation Bible School, I was standing at the pulpit, leading our closing ceremonies. We'd already sung songs, made crafts, engaged in Bible lessons, and devoured Mayfield ice cream. But we were all a bit surprised that the evening outdoor recreation activities had been cut short due to the sky opening up. We'd been in a period of drought for some time.

As I had done every night for the last several evenings, I asked the crowd of children (a little wet from wear) to tell me about their daily "God sighting"—how they had seen God at work on that particular day. Answers the previous nights had included smiles from friends and hugs from parents.

As soon as the question left my mouth, Jenna Kate Lee, daughter of dairy farmers, raised her hand high in the air. Since she was so enthused, I invited her to share her thoughts. Loud and clear this eight-year-old stated, "I thank God for the rain, because our corn needed it!"

I couldn't help but smile at that earnest and authentic praise to God. The rainstorm could have been viewed solely as an inconvenience for missing the games of the night, or even as being scary. But instead, this child recognized it as a true blessing. And in what might have been a chorus of *amens*, several other little children spoke up and said they were happy as well—as their parents' and grandparents' gardens had been hit hard by the recent drought. The adult and teenage volunteers nodded their heads in agreement. We were all truly thankful that God had opened the heavens—even if our heads had gotten a little soaked.

Isn't it glorious that these children, growing up in a farming community, know that we can toil all we want, but it is truly our God who drops the necessary dew from the heavens? We might prepare and fertilize the soil, and we might plant the seeds, but we know it is God who provides the rain that supplies our fields with water. God sustains life. His hand brings forth all life, and it is to Him we should devote our praise. Our work matters very little apart from Him.

Many times we view the everyday and ordinary as trivial or mundane. But there is something so extraordinary in the simple. I love how Zechariah 8:12 describes the process of raining in this way: "The heavens shall give their dew." This poetic and praise-giving phrase positions our minds to recognize the life-sustaining beauty of the everyday—and to see how our Creator designed all aspects of our natural world to thrive when every part works together. The soil, the rain, and the sunshine are all part of the process of growth.

Farm gal, let's not ever overlook God's marvelous workmanship. Instead, let's spend time each day, senses fully attuned, recognizing and praising God for all the splendid ways He works in our world.

We praise Him in the sun. And we praise Him in the rain.

FALLIN' A FLOOD CHALLENGE

"Fallin' a flood" is the Southern way of saying that the rain is unyielding. I challenge you to spend time each day focusing on the unyielding blessings that God drops from the heavens. He truly pours blessing upon blessing on our world, doesn't He? It is good for our souls to recognize these blessings and then praise Him for His workmanship.

Here are a few suggestions to get you in the habit of seeing God's blessings. You might choose one or more of these to incorporate into your daily routine.

- Start an evening gratitude journal. Write down a set number of items to give thanks for each night.
- State your blessings during your morning or afternoon or evening prayers.
- Set a daily alarm on your phone—and when it goes off, stop what you are doing and praise God for all the ways you see Him at work.
- Invite everyone at your dinner table to share one way they saw God at work during the day.
- Like drawing more than writing? Sketch your blessings in a journal each night.
- Stop, look, and praise. Every time you are stopped at a red light, praise God for one way you see Him at work.

JUNE

Blooming on the Farm

Each tree is known by its own fruit. For figs are not gathered from thornbushes, nor are grapes picked from a bramble bush.

LUKE 6:44

Farm gal, it's pep-talk time. We all need someone to speak truth and encouragement into our lives, so let me be your cheerleader today. Cheering you on with the Word of God.

It's nice to feel appreciated through words and actions—whether they come from our spouse, our child, our parent, our friend on social media, or the checker at the Dollar General. Whether we admit it aloud or not, we all crave this type of reassurance in our lives. Assurance that we matter and are loved *as is*. Not loved for our potential, but for our present self.

One of the reasons we crave this reassurance is because the world is so loud. It's constantly heralding ways we can improve. Just go on social media. Within a few minutes you'll see what I'm talking about. The push for us to become bigger and better. The push for self-growth. The push to rise and *then* be our best selves. The push that says we aren't made for small things. Push. Push. Push.

It's a bit of hogwash that brought me to tears. I was, as my friend Leah Davis would say, "Tore up six ways to Sunday." I cried myself to sleep one night reading online messages.

I have a hard-earned PhD. At one time my goal in life was very different from my present reality. At the crossroads of my personal journey, I turned down a job at a prestigious university so I could stay home with my kiddos and make peanut butter sandwiches on the daily. I had the potential for that "bigness" the world talks about. I was there! Standing at the apex, with a promise of reduced-price faculty football tickets and being called "doctor" for life.

And I passed on the opportunity.

The messages I was reading that evening on social media and blogs made me feel as if I had somehow wasted my life because I had climbed down from that lifestyle so I could be on call 24-7 to wipe baby bums.

Was my chosen path, the one I felt God called me to, unworthy? Was it too *small*? Had I derailed or somehow wasted my life because I wasn't going down the path leading to the biggest title?

I had some deep talks with God.

Had I prayed about my decisions? Check!

Had I found peace in my decisions based on following His guidance? Check!

Did I consult my husband? Check!

Well, there you go. God let me know that other opinions need not apply (except my spouse's, because God calls marriage a team).

My assurance is to rest in Him. There is no smallness, and there is no bigness. There is just *Him*. I can be holy and have a job at a big university. But I can also be holy and work within the home. What matters is that I go to Him—not the world—for approval of how to live my unique life.

We are to grow in God.

Now, pray tell, how can we grow in Him? I'm glad you asked.

Go out into your garden, your yard, or the neighborhood park. Take a gander at the plants. They are what they are, aren't they? They are exactly how God designed them to be when He first crafted the seeds that would go into the earth.

A pumpkin seed goes into the ground, and out pops a pumpkin.

A zinnia seed goes into the ground, and out blooms a zinnia.

It's really not a surprise that what is put into the earth is what blooms out of it. And God infused into each of us, when He created us in the womb, different seeds that would bloom. He didn't mess up with us either.

God put a seed of constant encouragement into one of my friends. And out blooms encouragement. God put a seed of teaching into another of my friends. And out blooms teaching. God loves uniqueness. He loves variety. As the expression goes, "It takes all kinds."

The plants out in my garden are content. They have an assurance that God didn't mess up when He made them. I never see a blackberry trying to be a soybean or a cucumber pining to be a tomato.

Farm gal, God loves you. He made you. He crafted you. He didn't make you a weed or a bramble. When you are in Christ, you will bloom all sorts of goodness.

God loves us all. The high-heels-wearing career woman. The barrel-racing cowgirl. The mama cleaning up spills. The grandmother line-dancing at the dance hall. The sports fanatic with the jersey on her back. And, by the way, all these descriptions could fit one woman. We aren't all just "one thing." We are different. We are varied. We are made up of many parts.

First Corinthians 12:4-6 says, "Now there are varieties of gifts, but the same Spirit; and there are varieties of service, but the same Lord; and there are varieties of activities, but it is the same God who empowers them all in everyone." How many times is the word *varieties* repeated in that scripture? Bunches. God created and likes variety. He created you, and He created me. He created us different. And He loves us all.

Our sameness is found in our purpose. First Corinthians 12:7 (NASB) says, "To each one is given the manifestation of the Spirit for the common good."

These verses from 1 Corinthians show us that God empowers us to live for Him *just as* He created us. We all have a role in His kingdom. His grand plan includes us being us. We don't have to grow "bigger" (as the world suggests) to reach that potential.

When the messages of the world start messing with your mind, take heed. This is a symptom showing you that you need to be filling up with God's truth, reading straight from the Bible. He is our ultimate encourager, our identity giver, and the one to whom we should be looking for acceptance (not the world).

He wants us to live God-centered lives and be content in our present stations. First Timothy 6:6 says, "Godliness with contentment is great gain." My sunflower is content being a sunflower. My rosebush seems to love being a rosebush. And God desires for you to be content being *you*.

Grow in Christ and not into the world. Growing is a good thing, but make darn tootin' sure you're growing because that's what God wants and not because of selfish ambition. We have the power to discern what is of God and what is of the world. Romans 12:2 says, "Do not be conformed to this world, but be transformed by the renewal of your mind, that by testing you may discern what is the will of God, what is good and acceptable and perfect."

Farm gal, live your life with the assurance that God crafted you to be unique. Go to Him, listen to Him about "what is good and acceptable and perfect" for your unique life, and find your assurance in Him and Him alone.

You will bloom brightest when your eyes are focused above.

WELL, I DECLARE!

Read the following verses to see what the Bible declares about you. Then write them down, repeat them, and thank God for declaring you *wonderful*.

> "God created man in his own image, in the image of God he created him; male and female he created them" (Genesis 1:27).

> "You formed my inward parts; you knitted me together in my mother's womb. I praise you, for I am fearfully and wonderfully made. Wonderful are your works; my soul knows it very well" (Psalm 139:13-14).

> "O LORD, you are our Father; we are the clay, and you are our potter; we are all the work of your hand" (Isaiah 64:8).

> "You are the body of Christ and individually members of it" (1 Corinthians 12:27).

> "He who had set me apart before I was born…called me by his grace" (Galatians 1:15).

> "We are his workmanship, created in Christ Jesus for good works, which God prepared beforehand, that we should walk in them" (Ephesians 2:10).

JULY

The Fourth on the Farm

Worthy are you, our Lord and God,
to receive glory and honor and power,
for you created all things,
and by your will they existed and were created.

REVELATION 4:11

It's the Fourth of July! Around here the cattle are relocated from one pasture to another to make room for parking cars and shooting fireworks; the Weed Eater whirls for three straight days to make the place spotless; and flags are hung on fence posts.

The Fourth on the farm is a big affair. Hundreds and hundreds of folks from around our community come to celebrate America. Our family, along with our neighbors and best friends – the Lee family, who own the dairy farm down the road, has been hosting this event for more than two decades, and we all work hard to put it together.

My husband and I were still high school sweethearts the first time I joined in on the fun. The tradition started with just a handful of people and grew over the years to a farm full of folks. But the core of the night has remained—food, fellowship, and fireworks.

The event isn't fancy. Just a slice of old-fashioned Americana. People start arriving as afternoon turns to evening and park their vehicles in the pasture. Children run in and out of the orchard and into the front field playing kickball, getting their faces painted, and throwing baseballs. It's not a night of bounce houses or electronics. We keep it simple.

We place the cobblers, pies, and cookies people bring on a wooden trailer draped with quilts and decorated with vases full of flowers and flags. The Community Action Group of Englewood makes funnel cakes. Barbeque is provided by our friends of Navarro's Smokehouse, or Tony Barnett lights up the grill. People sit and visit with friends on picnic blankets and lawn chairs. Our friend Blake curates a list of patriotic music that we listen to as we look out and see the red, white, and blue wave high on our farm.

The flag we gaze at is as big as the bucket of a front-end loader and was gifted to us by a member of the Lee family, a man in active service. The John Deere serves as a flag stand. The flag, which has seen time on foreign soil, is draped across the raised bucket of the loader. Mountains in the distance provide the backdrop. Sometimes a full moon even greets us with a show.

One of my favorite new traditions is to invite the children to come forward, in front of that flag-draped John Deere, and lead the crowd of hundreds in singing "The Star-Spangled Banner." It brings tears to my eyes to see these littles sing their hearts out about our great country while the crowd rises and places their hands over their hearts.

Thankfully we live in a part of America where the Pledge of Allegiance is said every morning at school and the national anthem is sung. These kids know the words by heart. And I'm sure most folks present, just like me, look at that flag and those kids and reflect on where we are and where we've been.

The Declaration of Independence was officially adopted by the Continental Congress on July 4, 1776. This break from Great Britain essentially founded the United States of America—a grand experiment of government based on liberty. It was one year later in Philadelphia, on July 4, 1777, that the celebration of Independence Day began. With what else? Fireworks.

Almost 100 years later, in 1870, Congress established Independence Day as a federal holiday. And we patriots have continued to celebrate this day ever since.

All across the United States celebrations take many different forms. But some common elements include wearing red, white, and blue; watching fireworks with family and friends; and taking time to think about and honor those who previously served or currently serve in our military.

We have lots of these brave veterans and active-duty military members who come celebrate with us on the farm. Truly, though, we're celebrating *them*. My grandfather, a World War II veteran, used to sit and watch the fireworks with us. B.T. Hutson lied about his age so he could join the military. At the age of 16, he was mobilized and served substantial time on the European front. He became recognized by *Yank*, a U.S. Army weekly magazine, as the youngest master sergeant in the army.

In our hearts, we celebrate men and women such as this. Our American heroes. We wave our flags with them on our minds.

That's part of our purpose in observing the Fourth of July—to celebrate the sacrifices that were made to preserve the liberty we enjoy now. A liberty fought for by the founders—and the citizens of each generation since.

Fifty years after the signing of the Declaration of Independence, Thomas Jefferson, one of the original writers of the document, was invited to attend the Independence Day celebration in Washington. He declined the invitation due to poor health. But he sent a reply expressing his appreciation for being invited and noting the importance of marking this day of official independence. In his last public letter he wrote,

> For ourselves, let the annual return of this day forever refresh our recollections of these rights, and an undiminished devotion to them.[1]

This turn of phrase reminds me of something our pastor said while sharing one of his yearly messages at our celebration of the Fourth on the farm.

With the Bible in one hand and a microphone in another, Brother Russ stood before the masses and reminded us that the First Amendment gives us the freedom to worship and the freedom to assemble. Our challenge is to celebrate our rights.

How can we celebrate and honor our freedom of worship? By worshiping.

How can we celebrate and honor our freedom of assembly? By assembling.

As Brother Russ pointed out, we are truly blessed to have these freedoms, which didn't come free. We must also take advantage of these liberties.

As fireworks shoot into the sky over the farmland and "God Bless America" plays for all to hear, we say, "Bless *You*, our God!" It is God whom we thank for our true liberty.

FIRE UP THE SMOKER

My best summer memories include eating good barbecue by the Hiwassee River. My dad, Doug, and his friends would stay up all night smoking the pork while my mom, Kim, made up the best sauce you'll ever taste. It's adapted from *Jack Daniel's Old Time Barbecue Cookbook*.[2] The only adaptation is that she left out the Jack Daniel's. But you can add it if you wish.

Kim's Barbecue Sauce

- 9 cups Worcestershire sauce
- 4 cups apple cider vinegar
- 1½ cups tomato juice
- ½ cup Tabasco sauce
- 2 quarts (8 cups) ketchup
- ½ cup garlic, minced
- 2 cups brown sugar
- 2 cups white sugar
- ½ cup paprika
- ½ cup black pepper
- 6 T. onion powder
- ½ cup salt
- Liquid smoke, to taste

Mix and simmer all ingredients together for 1 hour. Makes 1½ gallons. Enjoy!

JULY

Wildflowers on the Farm

We know that for those who love God all things work together for good, for those who are called according to his purpose.

ROMANS 8:28

In the Hundred Acre Wood is a meadow of wildflowers.

Think that's a line from the A.A. Milne classic? Nope, I'm just taking you on a trip to one of my favorite places on our farm. It's so idyllic that I nicknamed it after one of my favorite fictional locales. It's a place we go with our children for renewal. Fishing in the pond. Hiking in the forest. Swinging from the grape vines hanging off the trees. And watching our daughter make a fairy garden in the side of the massive mushroom-covered oak.

We all need places like this, don't we? A place of refreshment. The animals need these places as well. The Hundred Acre Wood on our farm isn't just for us—it is purposefully preserved to be a place of rejuvenation and conservation for creatures of all kinds.

God created the world to work together. One way this plays out is through the symbiotic, mutualistic relationship between flowering plants and pollinators.

Pollinators aren't featured in the song "Old MacDonald Had a Farm." Yet they are pivotal for the success of a farm, and for the world as a whole. Yes, little birds, bats, butterflies, bees, and other various insects and creatures are mighty important. The U.S. Forest Service says, "Virtually all of the world's seed plants need to be pollinated." They go on to caution, "Without pollinators, the human race and all of earth's terrestrial ecosystems would not survive."[1]

Did you realize your survival depends on pollinators? Bees need flowering plants for pollen. And those flowering plants need the bees to transport pollen from plant to plant so pollination (reproduction) can occur.

All the pollinators rely on plants. And the plants rely on them. They all rely on one another. They gain, and they give.

When my husband first started setting aside plots for wildflowers and native grasses, I thought he was just making our farm cute. What a perfect site for a photo shoot! Yes, that is what went through my mind. But then he explained to me that he was working with the local Natural Resources Conservation Service (NRCS) office to promote animal and plant conservation by planting these seeds.

Our wildflower and native grass fields are areas where pollinators can thrive. The birds and bees and butterflies flit about, gather pollen from the dazzling plants, and live their best pollinator lives. Turns out that these gorgeous plants the creatures visit aren't just a pretty face or the makings of a charming tabletop bouquet. Wildflowers nourish and provide life-giving sustenance.

But their gifts don't stop there! The wildflowers and native grasses grow and grow, providing a place for the birds to nest and small creatures to hide from predators.

These wildflowers just keep bestowing life, don't they?

Now we have flocks of turkeys that roam the Hundred Acre Wood. And herds of deer. And bunches of foxes, songbirds, rabbits, and squirrels.

As farmers we take lots of land and turn it into row crops or fields for grazing or plots for barns and shops. Unfortunately, this displaces native animals and plants. So it's important for us to set aside land for the propagation of God's creatures. It's holy work. It's doing our part to take care of God's earth.

His world never ceases to amaze me. The flowers. The bees. The bats. They all work together for good. Not just for beauty, but for our very survival. The apple we bite into only exists because the pollinators and flowers live out their purposes on earth.

Just like God created the ecological world to work together, He calls everything to work together—and we play a role in this as well.

You might not realize it, but you are like a wildflower. When you bloom or naturally exude the traits you have been given by Christ, you are bestowing life on others. Your genuine smile might be the lift someone needs to forge through their day. And similarly, when your fellow man blooms, you can gather God-sent bits of life that will sustain you.

Let's all be the wildflowers in our world and bloom brightly. Our very life comes from God, and when we abide in Him, we not only gain sustenance—we also bear fruit that nourishes others.

God causes everything to work together!

Plant wildflower seeds in your soul and your fields. You are helping the whole world go 'round.

BUSY AS A BEE

Want to establish your pollinator habitat? This list of native grasses and wildflowers was recommended to us by our friend Jason. He works with the NRCS and says this makes for an excellent cover establishment in our area.

Native Warm-Season Grasses

Side-oats grama

Little bluestem

Wildflowers

Black-eyed Susan

Smooth aster

Lanceleaf coreopsis

Partridge pea

Purple coneflower

Illinois bundleflower

Rattlesnake master

Indian blanket

Maximilian sunflower

Bergamot

Spotted beebalm

Gray-headed coneflower

PLANTING WILDFLOWERS AND NATIVE GRASSES

Call most any seed company and request that they premix the above varieties for you. Just tell them the size of the area you are planting. They might also offer different recommendations based on your geographic locale. The above list is best for our area in the southeastern United States.

After getting your seeds, till the soil lightly in your chosen plot. You might also consider spraying the ground with an herbicide that is not systemic (so there is no residual agent in the soil). This will eliminate any competition from weeds or grasses. In late spring, spread the seed mixture before a rain. Or water thoroughly after the seed is spread. Then watch the butterflies and other pollinators enjoy what you've provided for them.

⯌ JULY ⯌

Oh, Deere!

I have said these things to you, that in me you may have peace. In the world you will have tribulation. But take heart; I have overcome the world.

JOHN 16:33

My husband texted me a photo with a caption that read, "My day so far..." The photo featured the new John Deere cab tractor. But this wasn't a smiling farmer selfie. The tractor, with a front-end loader and a disc mower in the rear, was flipped on its side. Top of the cab all busted up.

Sadly, this wasn't one of our children's miniature toys. This was a real-deal Deere.

I called and frantically asked, "What? Are you okay?"

Turns out the driver of that particular tractor had looked over his shoulder at the rows of crops behind him and didn't notice the embankment in front of him. Down that embankment the tractor rolled.

Thankfully, the driver was uninjured. However, the cost of repairing the tractor was a jolt.

It's easy to ask, "Why me?" Have you had days like this? When you just want a do-over—or to pull out your hair and scream?

Farm gal, let's read one of God's promises.

You want the good news or the bad news first? Well, the two are a bit intertwined in this verse. "I have said these things to you, that in me you may have peace. In the world you will have tribulation. But take heart; I have overcome the world" (John 16:33).

Somehow I don't think a graphic tee with the words *You Gonna Have Trouble (John 16:33)* would sell super well at boutiques, but this is a true promise from God: Life will have troubles.

Yes, unfortunately we are assured we will have trials and tribulations. But the good, redeeming news is that Jesus has overcome the world. This means we will have days (and sometimes months and years) when trials come and come and come, but we have the promise that this is not our forever.

So what are we to do? How do we handle these earthly trials?

James (the half brother of Jesus) exhorts us to use trials to mature in our Christian faith. And, in a difficult-to-swallow pill of a verse, he tells us to count trials as joy.

> Count it all joy, my brothers, when you meet trials of various kinds, for you know that the testing of your faith produces steadfastness. And let steadfastness have its full effect, that you may be perfect and complete, lacking in nothing (James 1:2-4).

This passage packs a punch. One thing I notice is that James tells us it isn't unusual if we are facing trials. Although sometimes we think we are among the unlucky few, we must realize we all have our own rows to hoe. You aren't alone in the messiness of life. Everyone will face trials—including those who accept Christ into their lives.

I also notice that these trials James writes of aren't necessarily a consequence for having done something "bad." Yes, trials arise when you dig yourself into the hole of sin (see James 1:14-15), but the trials James is talking about in this situation are the side effects of life. You are familiar with those, aren't you? You get sick; the car doesn't start; the tractor ends up in a ditch; and so on.

You see, James says, "When you meet trials" (James 1:2). Quite literally this translates as "When you *fall into* trials."[1] You don't mean to fall into a ditch or down an embankment, do you? Farm gal, we *all* are going to fall into trials that test our faith. It is a given.

James also tells us we will face "trials of various kinds." This means many, varied. The trials we will face on this earth will fall into every single sort of category.

Little problems, like chipping our nails, and hard stuff, like cancer. We can't react to them all in the same way. But when we learn how to handle our nail chipping maturely, we will be better positioned to handle the big issues of life.

James tells us to use trials for growth (verse 4). Trials, he says, are opportunities to mature in our faith. Trials develop steadfastness—*hypomonē*, which is the Greek word for *endurance*.[2] We can endure more of the world's hardships if we keep our eyes on God. Trials help us keep practicing that drill. It's like exercise—we get a bit better at it each time, even if we don't want to face the treadmill.

I realize this isn't the sort of thing we can hash out in a short devotional reading. These ideas are big and require some changes to the heart. But I challenge you to read more about how trials can cause you to draw closer to God, learn how to fully rely on Him, and move with compassion toward others—thereby ministering with the love of Christ. Trials really can help us grow in Him.

Peter tells us that it will please God to no end when He sees us remain strong in our faith through trials. He says, "Now for a little while, if necessary, you have been grieved by various trials, so that the tested genuineness of your faith—more precious than gold that perishes though it is tested by fire—may be found to result in praise and glory and honor at the revelation of Jesus Christ" (1 Peter 1:6-7).

Farm gal, our tractor fell in the ditch, and we were out lots of money. I'm quite certain there were lots of words spewing out of my husband's mouth when he saw what had happened. Probably not much holy talk. But as the dust fell, in spite of the circumstance, he chose joy. You know why? Because no one was injured. In the grand scheme of life it was a very, very expensive hiccup—not a life-altering reality.

Here on the farm, in our family, we've faced those big hardships of life, including death at ages when it shouldn't happen—most notably my husband's sister, who passed away at the age of twenty, only three weeks before Perry and I got married. So Perry was able to internally categorize this particular farm-wreck as something we could handle. It was a big headache, but thankfully not a heartache.

Our previous experiences caused us to practice finding joy in our trial.

There are hardships that sink our knees into the dirt the minute they happen, aren't there? And we can stay in that dirt for a long time. We have to grieve and mourn and trust in the Lord and cry, cry, cry. And then there are hardships that can be overcome a bit easier. We must face those maturely and in as much of a Christlike manner as we can muster through God's grace.

As you go through your day, I challenge you to recognize the differences in the trials you face. Handle them accordingly. Work on maturing your faith in the little things, so that when the big things happen, you'll have the emotional energy and faith to walk with God through the heavy.

Farm gal, perfection is not found on this earth; trials will occur. And when they do, we must pray to God about how we can handle them (see James 1:5-8), then trust the path on which He directs us and believe that He is walking alongside us.

Sometimes this means we have to brush the dirt off our tush and get back in the saddle (or on another John Deere tractor)—knowing our final destination is where perfection reigns.

FINDING SWEETNESS IN THE SPICY

Prayer isn't always about asking for our circumstances to change—it's also about asking for our hearts to look differently at our circumstances. Spend time in prayer today about your trials. Pray this verse: "I consider that the sufferings of this present time are not worth comparing with the glory that is to be revealed to us" (Romans 8:18).

Now, finding sweetness in the spicy can be a challenge. But there is no denying the good taste of the sweet and hot mix of blackberries and jalapeños. When you find yourself in a jam, go ahead and make some!

Gardening is my friend Leighann's jam. She is also pretty good at making it (jam, that is)! My favorite is her blackberry jalapeño concoction. She grows her own peppers and often gets her blackberries from us.

(Note: You can't make this recipe without the proper water-bath canning supplies and being familiar with the water-bath canning process. So gather the supplies, read up on the process, and give this recipe a try.)

Leighann's Blackberry and Jalapeño Jam

6 cups fresh blackberries
2–3 jalapeños, seeded
1 box (1¾ oz.) pectin
7 cups sugar
12 half-pint Mason jars, cleaned and sterilized

Rinse the blackberries. Finely chop the jalapeños. Place the berries and peppers together in a pot. Bring mixture to a boil and stir continually. You'll be stirring until the end, so don't stop! Slowly add the pectin until it dissolves. Then slowly add the sugar. Keep on stirring! Boil for one minute. Now you can stop stirring and skim the foam off the top. Next, follow directions for water-bath canning. Filled Mason jars should be processed in the water bath for 10 minutes. Enjoy!

JULY

Bear on the Farm

You shall eat and be full, and you shall bless the LORD your God for the good land he has given you.

DEUTERONOMY 8:10

Hunter called it the "Ghost of the Corn Patch."

I blamed it on Bigfoot.

Some folks scoffed and said it was a raccoon.

But the scat of the animal proved it to be a bear.

This was verified by the Tennessee Wildlife Resources Agency and our neighbor Jarrod, a man of the cloth who is not prone to lying or exaggerating. If he says it's a bear, you can rest assured that it is a bear.

This creature was coming into our sweet-corn patch, in the dead of the night, and pulling up entire corn stalks. From the root!

We'd arrive in the early June mornings at the patch just across the street from our farmhouse to pick sweet corn. But we'd be met with discarded cobs eaten plumb in two. Raccoons can't bite corncobs in two! This was the job of a grizzly-toothed creature.

Corn stalks were uprooted and thrown all around. Turns out the bear would sit in the soil and start picking up each stalk within reach. It was a midnight game of folly. He left tracks and scat everywhere. Then he'd disappear.

Perry called the TWRA to come set a trap. The corn bandit needed to be caught.

Have you ever seen a bear trap? It is mighty big. The size of a small truck, except oblong. Freddy, the TWRA agent, pulled the trap underneath the wild cherry tree at the edge of the corn patch. He hung a bag of sardines at the entrance to the trap. Then he placed another bag of sardines deep inside it. The bear, focused on feeding his belly, would walk into the trap and eat the first bag of sardines. But then, since he's a bear, he'd go for round two and walk to the back of the trap. Unbeknownst to him, grabbing for that second bag of sardines would trigger the door of the trap to shut. Then the hungry creature would be safely relocated to the nearby Cherokee National Forest. At least, that was the plan.

We woke up early the next morning and eagerly anticipated seeing our catch. But nothing. No bear in the trap. Only more corn stalks uprooted. More scat. More tracks.

This went on for days.

Weeks.

A month passed, and that trap was still empty.

This is when we developed the nickname "Ghost Bear."

Catching a bear is harder than you might imagine. We adjusted our bait plan. I threw in a dead trout my son had caught at the Tellico River, and I poured out an entire Mason jar of our prized honey. Based upon my readings of *Winnie-the-Pooh*, I was certain this fish-honey combination would be irresistible.

Still nothing.

We heard bears like honey buns, and so we sacrificed several boxes of them and put them into the trap.

Still nothing.

Then I heard about bears coming to campsites when bacon was being cooked over the open fire. So, one evening I cooked the bear a plate of bacon on our stove and drove it up to the trap.

Still nothing. This bear wasn't biting. He just really loved our sweet corn!

Some say he detected our smell and that's why he stayed away from the trap. But I'm not buying that because we had been all over that corn patch and *that* sure didn't deter him from eating our crop.

Finally, the end of summer arrived—and that meant the end of our corn season. Which is exactly when the bear stopped visiting.

So, the trap was removed.

Bearless.

Maybe it really was Bigfoot. He would be smarter than a bear, right? More elusive. It's the natural conclusion.

Bear or Bigfoot, he sure did steal a lot of our crop this summer, but he also brought us lots of corn-picking fun. Our load was lighter as we spent time finding the tracks. Our time passed quickly as we discovered new areas where the corn had been pulled. And plotting out the best food to use for trapping the bear became not only fun for us, but also for all our friends on social media. The toil of the summer was made lighter by all the laughter.

> You shall eat and be full, and you shall bless the Lord your God *for the good land he has given you* (Deuteronomy 8:10).

It turns out that although the deed to the land has our name on it, God gave this land to the creatures too. And this animal sure was enjoying all that sweet corn God had us grow for him.

He was satisfied.

God provides for all of us, doesn't He? He provides food for us to eat. And He provides laughter-filled situations that sustain our souls with joy. Even when we toil.

WELL, I'LL SAY!

Let's praise God for all the ways He satisfies our needs (and the needs of bears/Bigfoot). Grab a piece of paper and see how many blessings you can write down in five minutes. I bet that list will be ripe with evidence of God's goodness in your life.

AUGUST

Corn Shucking on the Farm

Let us consider how to stir up one another to love and good works, not neglecting to meet together, as is the habit of some, but encouraging one another, and all the more as you see the Day drawing near.

HEBREWS 10:24-25

My dear friend came over last Tuesday, and we sat on my front porch in the golden August sunshine, shucking sweet corn for nearly two hours. Our babes played nearby amid the pile of cobs. She and I chatted about nonsense and deep matters of the heart. At one point I had to wipe away salty tears while I recounted some recent events. She offered godly wisdom and cheeky comments.

Isn't that how it is with our gals? Talking about everything under the sun. I taught her how to eat corn straight off the cob; she taught me how to cream it.

We were pretending to be homesteaders, although we both prefer modern conveniences. Our conversation felt nostalgic—like we should have been wearing cotton aprons tied around our waists, and our husbands should have been out raising a barn or hunting big game.

Don't the days of old seem to have been ripe for the growing of community? Built into the old-fashioned routines of life were pockets of time for females to tend to their work and children. Time to chat. To build relationships. To have companionship. Connecting with nature and people.

Do we really make time for tasks like this anymore? Sitting side by side while breaking green beans, piecing together a quilt, or picking blackberries? Sure, nowadays we share recipes online and funny memes via text, but I fear that when we relegate our time together to coffee or lunch that we sometimes miss the delight built into life a century ago—the sharing of the workload, emotions, and laughter.

That August day Leighann and I were stocking our freezers for the winter. We were working so our families' bellies would be full of vegetables my husband had painstakingly cultivated. So we could bite into a fresh reminder of the juiciness of summer on a dark winter night. But most importantly—so we could fill our souls. Sitting side by side, breathing in the fresh air while doing a mindless task that was anything but meaningless.

Women need women. We need to meet together to encourage one another. To listen to heartache and happiness. To laugh and giggle. To refresh each other so we can continue putting our best selves forward.

I was revitalized while sitting alongside this friend of mine. Each of us pouring out our thoughts as we shucked corn and removed the silk. It was like we were pulling back the layers of our lives as we pulled back the layers of those cobs.

Today's lifestyle leaves very little margin for the true cultivation of friendship. We are too busy going from one task to the next. We've followed the gospel of productivity instead of the gospel of availability. We need to set aside time to just sit, in an unhurried fashion, in the proximity of godly women. Soaking in their presence, reaping their advice and love.

Hebrews 10:24-25 says, "Let us consider how to stir up one another to love and good works, not neglecting to meet together, as is the habit of some, but encouraging one another, and all the more as you see the Day drawing near." The author of Hebrews was writing to an audience facing hard times.

"Hard times" can have many different meanings. On the extreme end is violent religious persecution, which the audience of Hebrews faced. For us, hard times might look like a house fire, becoming a widow, or even experiencing a pandemic that changes every sector of our lives. Even smaller problems—like missing a vacation due to a child being sick—can also bring us down. Any type of strife can threaten our relationship with Christ.

The book of Hebrews tells us that we must meet together and encourage one another. We can better face hard times when we have godly friends to encourage us and help us ensure that we don't allow our relationship with the great I Am to fracture.

One thing my sun-washed afternoon spent shucking corn taught me is that just as much as I need food for nourishment, I also need godly friendship for my own renewal. That time together with Leighann helped me stock my freezer for the winter, but it also stocked my heart with encouragement.

How can you work some gal time into your life? Maybe you have some corn to shuck. Invite a pal to come sit on your porch and work beside you. At the very least, make a point to call a friend this week. Have a real voice-to-voice chat. Even if the conversation just lasts five minutes, it will bring life to your heart.

AWW, SHUCKS!

Although a gazillion ways exist to put up corn—that is, prepare fresh corn for the freezer—I have found this method works best for my family. It's simple and tastes great. Prepare the corn, pop it in the freezer, and eat throughout the fall, winter, and spring. Just make sure you use freezer bags and not lighter storage bags.

Putting Up Corn

Shuck the corn and remove the silk. No washing or blanching required. Put 4 to 6 ears in each gallon-sized freezer bag. Extract air from the freezer bags and zip them shut. Place the sealed bags in the freezer. When you're ready to eat the corn, remove the ears from the freezer and place them in already boiling water for around 5 to 7 minutes. Seriously, it's that easy. Enjoy!

AUGUST

Getting Away from the Farm

In all toil there is profit,
but mere talk tends only to poverty.

PROVERBS 14:23

My family loves to travel. In fact, my oldest declines ice cream money for school; he'd prefer extra change go into our jar designated for adventures.

Maybe your family likes going to the movies or sporting events, or maybe you use your extra money for home fun like the latest technology. We all like treats in life, don't we? And all of us must make choices on how to allot our personal finances. It's part of "adulting." Many of us have budget categories for saving, tithing, giving, and necessities.

Yes, the necessities of life—like toilet paper, prescriptions, mortgage payments, and food for our fridge—take up most of our income. But in addition to paying for the necessities, we often get to put some extra profits toward the wants of life. Our family likes to use extra profits and spare change for savings and together time.

One way we build up our change jar is through chores. Yep, my children know that if they talk about wanting to go somewhere, they'd better get to work to help us pay for the adventure.

When my oldest was eight, he spent weeks of his summer in the 100-degree Tennessee heat of the sweet-corn patch, picking corn off the stalks. He also spent many afternoons in the fall harvesting pumpkins. Can you believe that my child and his teenage cousin would pick (by hand!) 100 dozen ears of corn at a time?

My oldest wasn't the only one who lent a hand to the labor that year. My five-year-old daughter helped in the field (somewhat) and was my farm-stand assistant selling produce. The toddler offered moral support. It was a family affair.

We had a goal in mind. A goal decided upon by the children.

Disney World!

Many, many, many ears of corn later (and after paying off the cost of the seed and additional labor), we stood before the Cinderella Castle in the Magic Kingdom. We rode Space Mountain, and my son ate all the Mickey ice cream bars he wanted. The hard work of my kiddos led to a magical experience for our entire family. They also learned a valuable lesson, as Proverbs 14:23 says: "In all toil there is profit, but mere talk tends only to poverty."

My kids could talk all they wanted about getting the reward of Disney World, but unless they got their rears in gear they weren't going to receive this treat. At least, that's what I thought the lesson would be from this experience. However, I learned quite a bit from the process myself. Not necessarily about corn, but about how we all have important but somewhat different roles in the family of God.

In 1 Corinthians 12 the apostle Paul talks about the body of Christ. As Christians we are members of God's body. We might say that Christ is our leader, and together with Him we form God's "tribe." In this tribe we all have our own roles (spiritual gifts). All roles are equally important, but different. In our varying roles, we work together toward common goals. One of our goals as Christians is to disciple others. This is so as many people as possible can know Christ and live eternally in heaven with Him.

Let's see how this concept played out in the corn patch.

This past summer the Philpott Tribe had the goal of getting to Disney World. We had to work together with the common goal in mind. Each member of our tribe had different, but important, roles. Sometimes our roles overlapped, but it was obvious that we all had gifts to use in the endeavor.

My father-in-law ordered the seeds and planned out the field. Perry got the ground ready, planted the seeds, and made sure the corn was growing. Don't we, as the body of Christ, need those who first break the ground and sow the seeds and take care while the seeds are young and growing?

After the planting and growing, we need harvesters. Our harvesters were myself, my children, and our farm workers (including our teenage cousin Hunter). Many days the harvest work would make us grow weary. On occasion my son Titus would bemoan the fact that his wrists were sore from twisting off the corn. But Hunter, whose gift is definitely encouragement, would make the day fun and remind my Titus of the reward ahead. Don't we, as the body of Christ, need encouragers when our work gets wearisome?

Sometimes sudden rain showers would arrive while we were picking the corn. It was during those downpours that my son would rally and prevail. His favorite time to work was when the flood was a fallin'. Don't we, as the body of Christ, need disciples willing to work in the hard times?

But we couldn't just harvest the crop and then let it sit still. Nope. We needed to spread the news that we had corn for sale so we could share the crop with others. That's where my daughter Sophie, our cousin Hailee, and I excelled. I spread the news on social media, and then we sat on the roadside serving customers. Don't we, as the body of Christ, need those who can spread the good news of the gospel by interacting with others?

Yes, we all had different gifts and roles in the cornfield, but we were all working toward the same goal—Disney World. The hope of the reward ahead kept us all motivated. The promise of the future made our load seem lighter. We could look ahead from the cornfield and imagine our vacation.

As Christians we know the profit of our faith and works is far better than seeing that castle in the Magic Kingdom. Our heavenly reward is far more spectacular. We will not only get to see the streets of gold, but to live there as well. And we have the hope that we will have helped disciple others who will enjoy that place too.

That's pretty incredible, isn't it?

In Christ's body we all have different gifts, and we should celebrate our various roles as we work toward our common goal—abiding in Christ and knowing our reward is eternal. And heaven will be more spectacular than anything Walt Disney could ever have imagined!

EARN YOUR CORN

One of my dearest friends, Chrissi, makes the best creamed corn around. She picks dozens and dozens of corncobs. Prepares the creamed corn. Freezes it. And enjoys it all winter. She calls it a labor of love. Below is her recipe.

Tip: The little old lady who first told Chrissi of this method advised that the corn never touch metal, so she should only use a glass pan and wooden spoons. Is this true? Who knows? But Chrissi says she isn't going to mess with a good thing!

Chrissi's Creamed Corn

Shuck, de-silk, and rinse a dozen or more fresh ears of corn. Cut off corn from the cob with a knife. Be careful not to cut too close to the cob—you just want to "nick" the tops of the kernels. This means you will cut off the top half of the kernels while leaving the bottom part on the cob. Then use the knife to scrape the remaining corn off the cob. Repeat until no more juice can be removed.

Mash the corn with your hands a few times in the bowl. Then put corn in a clear glass baking dish and warm up in the oven (at about 250°). Heat until barely warm (around 20 minutes). Let cool. If you're not eating right away, place cooled corn in a freezer bag and freeze.

When serving, thaw the corn and add butter, salt, and pepper to taste. Bake in the oven until bubbly. Serves 4-6. Enjoy!

AUGUST

Fowl on the Farm

Know well the condition of your flocks,
and give attention to your herds.

PROVERBS 27:23

My daughter Sophie once took the concept of caring for animals to the extreme. She puckered up and kissed a chicken.

That hen wasn't happy with the unwanted advances and bit her. Or pecked her. I'm not exactly sure what you call a chicken kiss gone wrong (there was blood!). Maybe "fowl play"?

God tells us to pay attention to our herds, but that doesn't mean we have to give them hugs and cuddles. Rather, as caretakers of our herds and flocks, we must make sure their needs are met and they are safe.

We have herds of cattle on our farm and a few flocks of birds. The chickens give us eggs. The guinea fowl are our wandering pest control (they eat bugs like ticks and mosquitoes). The ducks swim around our pond and look cute. And the turkey, well, he was relocated to another farm (you'll read the rest of that story in a bit). We care for our animals by knowing their conditions and providing for any needs.

In agrarian societies of old, taking care of the flocks and herds was necessary for survival; people's lives and economic situations were dependent upon taking good care of the animals. The fowl were important sources of food and kept insects away. Herds provided milk, meat, and fibers for clothing and blankets.

In modern society, most of us are not dependent upon the sheep in our pastures for providing us a closet full of clothing or the chickens in our henhouse for providing us breakfast. Yet we are still caretakers.

Our caretaking in modernity looks a little different though, doesn't it? We have careers, households to manage, and a host of other duties. But, just like the call to care for our flocks, God desires for us to tend to our responsibilities.

This can be hard. Many of us are tasked with multiple roles. Sometimes that caretaking can be easy—giving a sweet child who has a boo-boo a little kiss. Other times the caretaking can be challenging—we might have teenagers who need a long chat and guidance to help bandage a broken heart.

What I find interesting is that the advice God gives us to care for our herds and flocks can also help us care for our households. Proverbs 27:23 says, "Know well the condition of your flocks, and give attention to your herds."

Replace the words *flocks* and *herds* with the names of those who are in your charge. Maybe a child. A spouse. A friend. A family member. Try it.

Do you see where I'm going? Our directive is to *know* them and *pay attention* to them.

That's a pretty good basis for caretaking. But what does all this require?

HOW TO TELL IF AN EGG IS FRESH

An important aspect of gathering fresh eggs is being able to test their freshness. Titus is great at doing this when he, Sophie, and Beckham collect the eggs. We want to guarantee that an egg hasn't been hiding under the straw for a month!

How to test? It's easy. Titus says to place the egg in a basin of water. If the egg sinks to the bottom, you know it is super fresh. If it stands up, you should use it very soon. But if it floats, toss that egg in the trash.

Time. Observation. A relationship. Diligence. Follow-through.

Let's give it a whirl, shall we?

I *know* my daughter, the one who kissed a chicken, can become cranky if she doesn't get her sleep. So, part of my caretaking duty is making sure she eats dinner, hears a bedtime story, receives lots of love, and is put down for a full night of sleep. I *know* my daughter, and I *pay attention* to her.

I *knew* my son—who, at the age of three, asked God to strike our turkey dead—was extremely fearful of the turkey's constant attempts at flogging him. So, my caretaking duty was to ensure the safety of my son. We got rid of the attack turkey by selling him to a farm who needed an attack turkey. I *know* my son, and I *pay attention* to his needs.

See how this works with people in our charge?

But *knowing* and *paying attention* can also help us prioritize our other responsibilities—even household chores that we might tackle alone or with assistance.

I have a love-hate relationship with my washer and dryer. I *know* that if I don't use them, our clothes will be dirty, and eventually we will have nothing to wear. So I keep a supply of laundry detergent on hand and make myself (and my family) use our laundry room. We need clean clothes, so we must wash. I *know* this, and I *pay attention* to the status of our laundry. It's a form of contemporary caretaking.

I *know* that if my refrigerator and pantry are bare, our family will not eat. So, my husband or I go to the grocery store for modern-day hunting and gathering. Food is necessary for our bodies to survive. I *know* this, and I *pay attention* to the status of our food supply.

PUCKER UP

God calls us to be caretakers of this earth and our responsibilities upon it. Whether we show care with a kiss or by whipping up a meal, we should all try our best to take care of whatever flocks and herds God has placed within our lives.

But I do caution you, chickens just need water and feed—that's pretty much it. So save your puckering up for someone else!

AUGUST

Rest on the Farm

[The tree's] leaves were beautiful and its fruit abundant, and in it was food for all. The beasts of the field found shade under it, and the birds of the heavens lived in its branches, and all flesh was fed from it.

DANIEL 4:12

As the sun rises the rooster begins crowing, the cattle start grazing, and the llamas frolic in the fields.

As the day continues our guinea fowl wander around our farmhouse—the backyard in the morning, the side yard around noon, and the front yard in the afternoon. They peck the bugs but also take time to find a spot underneath the rosebushes or on a bed of leaves for a little slumber during the day.

When the sun is high in the sky, the cattle slowly gather under the shade tree. The entire herd is shielded from the heat by the leaves. The horse and donkey plop down in the pasture to rest their legs. Our porch cat dozes, all curled up.

At sunset the chickens and the guinea fowl find a place to roost. Some fly to barn rafters or tree limbs, while others go into the henhouse. The ducks find their pondside nests. And the bats—well, they awaken from their daytime slumber, stretch their wings, and soar through the starry sky.

The rhythms of the animals on the farm are fascinating. But I've not noticed any of them needing a clock to tell them when to slumber. Instinct is their guide. All the farm animals have periods of time when they are awake and periods when they rest.

Do you have rhythms of rest?

God created us with certain needs, and sleep is one need we must meet daily.

In today's busy world we often sacrifice sleep for productivity. At sunset we don't start our journey to the roost, but instead try to catch our second wind. Taking time to sit or let our mind wander—even for a second—is something we ordain as lazy.

In a "Get it, girl" culture we sometimes receive the message that the hustle is the only way. The ladder must be climbed. We must "take control" of our time—which usually adds more to our calendar instead of less. But I feel this message is dangerous, because it's not "our time," is it? It's *God's* time. And when we don't follow His directives, we wither.

God, who created us in His perfect image, crafted us. And He gave us the innate need for rest. He is our designer; He knows His creation. Our fruitfulness is dependent upon us following His plan for our lives. To suggest otherwise is heretical and self-destructive. Rest is a gift God designed us to need, because He cares for us.

Psalm 127:2 says, "It is in vain that you rise up early and go late to rest, eating the bread of anxious toil; for he gives to his beloved sleep."

Beloved. Isn't that a lovely name for us? And God wants us to accept and embrace this gift. Not to live a life in angst and anxiousness. Not to constantly fight the rhythmic need He designed in our bodies. He takes care of us and blesses us—even in our sleep.

My son Beckham used to fight sleep. At two he still needed a nap but wouldn't easily settle. I tried everything. Then one day we noticed that a rhythm was happening outside the bedroom window. Each and every day, at the time I would take my son into his room for his nap, we'd see a herd of cattle mosey over to the shade tree. They'd lay down and still their bodies.

"See, even the cows need their rest!" I said.

Soon this became our rhythm. We'd giggle at the sight of the napping herd and read a book or two, and then my little son would drift off as he gazed out the window, watching the cattle have their moo, moo, nap, nap time.

I told Beckham all God's creatures need rest. And I reminded him that he's one of God's most beloved and treasured creatures. There is a time for rest and a time for play.

You are beloved by God. You are one of His most loved and treasured creations. His magnum opus. You, too, have a time for work, a time for play, and a time for rest.

Embrace a rhythm of rest and know that all God's creatures—including you—require sleep. Don't fight it. Instead, rest in that gift.

MOO, MOO, NAP, NAP

Farm gal, you might be the mother of a small child or a child with special needs, or perhaps you take care of an elderly family member. I know rest is what you crave, but it is not as easily accessible for you. I get it. I'm a mom of four and haven't fully slept in ten years. Let's pray that we will find pockets of time to rest our weary bodies and that we will feel no guilt for taking time to embrace those elusive quiet moments.

Heavenly Father, I pray that I will accept this gift of sleep that You have provided to all of us. Sometimes I fight sleep, dwelling on anxious thoughts and to-do lists. Help me quiet these thoughts. Help me decide what needs to be pruned or adjusted within my life so I can rest. Amen.

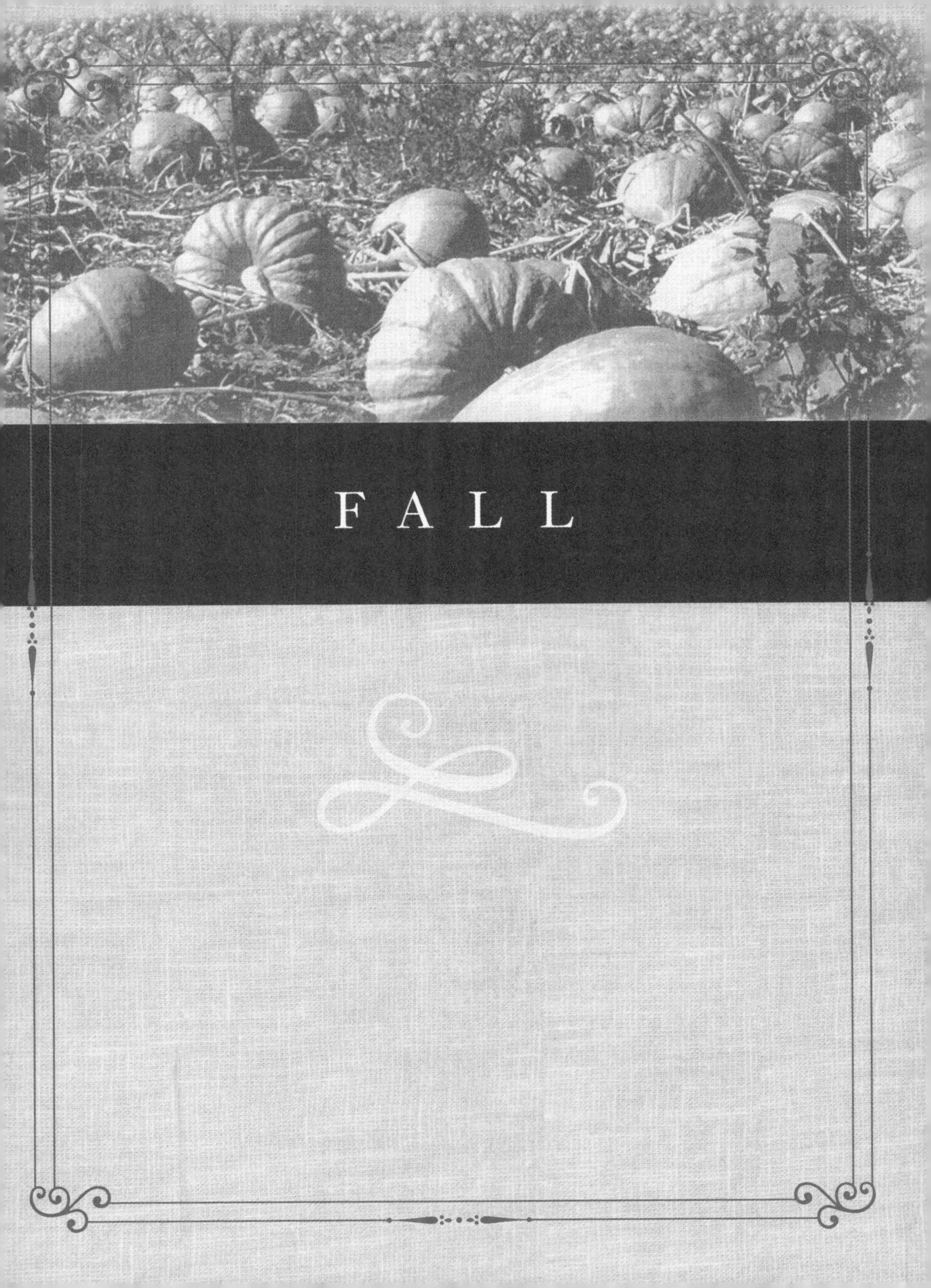

FALL

Welcome Fall

All at once, summer collapsed into fall.

OSCAR WILDE

Smell backyard campfires? See the leaves falling off the trees? Taste the apple cider? Hear the silence of the night? Fall is here, and farm tasks are plenty in this season of harvest! Some of our fall tasks here on the farm include…

- harvesting crops
- chopping corn silage
- performing maintenance for planting equipment
- sowing cover crops
- weaning cattle

Farm gal, this fall let us savor the food, the friends, and the Savior. Let's spend some time this week scribbling out our fall intentions. Of course, just like on a farm, plans change. It's okay if our intentions don't all garner check marks. The best-laid plans often go awry, as the poet Robert Burns noted. Let's enjoy the ride!

What might you like to…

- *plant in your life*? What can you sow?
- *cultivate in your life?* What can you tend to that's already growing?
- *prune in your life?* What do you need to discard or trim a bit?

PICK A SCRIPTURE

What scripture can you meditate on for the fall season?

PRAY A PRAYER

Heavenly Father, may we experience the blessings of the harvest as we thank You, the Lord of the harvest, for your mercies, grace, and love.

SEPTEMBER

Apple Picking on the Farm

Be patient, therefore, brothers, until the coming of the Lord. See how the farmer waits for the precious fruit of the earth, being patient about it, until it receives the early and the late rains. You also, be patient. Establish your hearts, for the coming of the Lord is at hand.

JAMES 5:7-8

We have a small orchard on the east side of our farmhouse. A few apple trees, pear trees, and peach trees stand firm in the soil. They are less than a dozen in number but are perfect for playing hide-and-seek or building forts or just wandering in the spring and admiring the blossoms.

When the late-summer harvest comes, my soul stirs with thanksgiving and amazement as I pluck apples from the limbs. Not due to the taste of the fruit, but from sheer awe that my hands are the ones picking apples from these particular trees.

My husband and I planted this small orchard when we were high school sweethearts. For him it was nothing more than a love of planting that led him to plant those fruit trees in what was then the yard of his childhood home. For me it was just a date. I was over at his house and helped him shovel the dirt into the holes he'd dug into the earth.

It wasn't a grand plan. We had no aspirations for these trees. I was just assisting my love, and he was just being himself. He's always loved planting things just to watch them grow.

The trees didn't bear fruit when we were in high school, and they didn't bear fruit when we were in college. But sometime during our marriage the trees matured, and we began gathering fruit in the front yard of what is now our home.

Truthfully, neither of us ever imagined that our youthful love would last, mature, and then one day lead to four children who would eat the fruit of what our teenage hands had planted. We had been caught up in the moment, unaware that we were making an impact for a future generation.

It can be like this with our spiritual lives as well—making a difference with our choices, but not truly realizing in the moment the long-term impact we will have. Sometimes we go along, just living day to day, and don't realize that the seed of God's Word we are unknowingly spreading will impact a future generation. Each day our actions and words and responses have the possibility to stir the heart of someone toward Christ—whether we interact with a person in real life at the grocery store or share a post on social media that another person reads.

When I was planting those trees, I wasn't looking ahead or planting with a purpose—I was just being the girlfriend of a farmer and helping him with his task. But regardless of intent, I was still helping give life to the roots and planting something that would one day bear fruit.

As Christians we don't always have to have a five-point plan or a calendar full of "help people" events to do the Lord's work. We do His work of discipleship all the time. We people of the Lord spread seeds everywhere we go and often have no idea we are helping in the germination of someone else's spiritual growth.

We are all missionaries, aren't we? Being a missionary isn't just an occupation; it's a way of life. And foreign service need not be required. We are called to live out our daily life loving God and loving others.

One reason we might not realize we are stirring up seeds of growth is because it can take a long, long time for a seed to develop and bear fruit. And when we don't see immediate results, we don't realize we are making a difference. But we are.

In an ancient Jewish text, there is a story of a fig tree being planted by a man of old age. The story says that a Roman emperor walked by and laughingly asked the gray-haired man if he thought he was going to live long enough to eat the fruit from the tree. The old man replied, "I was born into a world flourishing with ready pleasures. My ancestors planted for me, and now I plant for my children."[1]

We patiently wait. Sometimes we plant and know that in about 90 days we will harvest a crop. But other times we plant and wait and wait and wait. Knowing we might not ever be the ones to partake of the fruit, but someone else will. And that's a worthy cause! We plant expectantly, and we wait patiently for the marvelous work of growing and bearing.

We should carry a similar mindset regarding discipleship. Jesus asks us to work together for the Lord of the harvest (see Matthew 9:38). As Christians we don't always know when what we plant will bear fruit; neither do we know who the recipient of that fruit will be. However, we are asked to be disciples and work together for the good of God's kingdom.

We have to surrender our worldly desire for immediacy and instead draw into the godly attribute of patience.

Know that the seed you are planting right now (whether knowingly or unknowingly) might just mean that someone else will be included in the harvest of heaven. An eternal place where we can all enjoy fruit off the tree (see Revelation 22:2). Now that's fruit worth waiting for!

Keep planting—knowing you might not see the results, but having faith that your work is making a difference for generations and generations to come.

ALL IN GOOD TIME

Our friend Rachel makes the best applesauce I've ever tasted. We love eating her applesauce plain or mixed in an apple pie. Gather some apples and make this delicious treat that you can preserve to eat throughout the year.

(Note: If you want to preserve the applesauce, you'll need the proper water-bath canning supplies and a familiarity with the water-bath canning process. So gather the supplies, read up on the process, and give this recipe a try. Or you can whip up this recipe and eat and share the results immediately!)

Rachel's Homemade Applesauce

12 apples
½ cup water
1 T. lime juice
¼ cup brown sugar
½ cup of sugar
⅛ tsp. nutmeg
¼ tsp. vanilla
½ tsp. cinnamon

Peel and cut up the apples. Place apples, water, and lime juice into a saucepan and cook over medium heat for 15 minutes until apples are soft. Once the apples have softened, put them into the blender and blend to your desired texture. Return the apples to the saucepan and add the remaining ingredients, stirring it all together. Bring the apple mixture to a boil, remove from heat, and promptly pour it into Mason jars. If you'd like to preserve the applesauce, follow directions for water-bath canning. Enjoy!

SEPTEMBER

Fugitive on the Farm

Whoever sows sparingly will also reap sparingly, and whoever sows bountifully will also reap bountifully. Each one must give as he has decided in his heart, not reluctantly or under compulsion, for God loves a cheerful giver.

2 CORINTHIANS 9:6-7

I begged Perry not to turn him in to the police.

We could hide him out in the woods.

We could get him a plane ticket out of the country.

But let's not turn him in to the sheriff.

Ever hear something come out of your mouth that just doesn't make much sense? That's what was happening to me. I never expected to beg to be an accomplice in the crime of harboring a fugitive.

The story starts back in the spring. A young couple showed up on the farm ready to work. We didn't know much about their background, but the gal was associated with a friend of a friend, so we figured that was enough vetting.

The man started working on the farm, and the woman started making a home down the road. He helped bring in the hay, pick the corn, tend the cattle, and all other types of jobs. He showed lots of promise; it is difficult to find able and hard workers willing to handle the long hours and—let's be honest—my father-in-law's "get to work" style of leading. Only the strong survive around here! But he was making the cut.

Evidently the man started asking Perry about things of heaven, and Perry took the opportunity to pick corn side by side with him and talk about God. He then invited the young couple to go to church with us.

The couple agreed.

We started taking them to church. Throughout the summer they'd load up in our vehicle, along with our young kids, and we'd go sit on the same pew. Afterward we'd have lunch together and talk about all sorts of things. A little bit of Christian pride (never a good thing) swelled in my soul. Perhaps we were helping these folks get a fresh start.

But that notion was busted up when we got word that the guy was a felon. And not just any felon, mind you. He was not a reformed felon. He was not a former felon. He was a felon wanted by the sunny state of Florida.

Wanted.

A runaway.

Warrant out for his arrest.

Yep, we'd unknowingly been harboring a felon on our farm. And feeding him Sunday dinner to boot.

My immediate reaction was to hide him out in the woods and let him just keep on hiding. A sane first response, right?

"But he's not a murderer, Perry!" I found myself saying, trying to convince him. "If he's going to know Jesus, he needs to stay around here."

Perry explained that a big part of accepting Jesus was turning away from your former ways. Knowingly being a wanted felon without turning yourself in is not a great way to get started on trying to live a life like Jesus. Making amends with our past is part of repentance. And this guy, although nice and friendly, had a little issue that needed to be reconciled.

It was hard on both Perry and me, hearing that this man was a wanted felon. But there is a fine line between helping and enabling. And harboring a fugitive had crossed the line into enabling.

My emotions swung between sadness at what was going to happen and anger. We'd put our children at risk; we'd been lied to; and our generosity had been taken advantage of by two people who knew full well they were hiding out on the farm and trying to escape the reality of their former choices.

It's easy to give when we know that our "gift" of compassion or a helping hand will be used well. But what happens when we discover that the gift we extend isn't being used in a manner to our liking? That's the spiritual fallout I was facing.

I look back now and see how we must practice the hard habit of giving without expectation. My husband reminded me that if God calls our hearts to offer assistance to someone (and He had called us to befriend this couple), we should follow His calling. We must do as God calls us and sow bountifully—even when we don't know if the seed will be received well.

We don't know the Lord's ways. While in prison this young man might have time to understand the call to Jesus that had stirred in his heart—or he might disregard it and go out and commit another crime. We can't know. But no matter what happens, when we are called to sow, we must sow.

God doesn't call us to enable, but He does call us to present His Word. And we must trust that it is God who does the heart work.

I SWAN

Background checks are part of most hiring procedures. Truthfully though, we all need to do a background check on our own lives. Do you have something in the past you need to reconcile? Is something

WHEN IS THE WATERMELON RIPE FOR THE PICKING?

Look at the little squiggly tendril on the vine. A good predictor that a watermelon is ripe is when the tendril has turned from green to brown. You can also check the underside of the watermelon; the ground spot will have turned from white to yellow or brown. Finally, thump the watermelon. If you thump it and it is soft, it is not ready. You want it to be firm and tight, producing a good solid *thump*.

It's best to harvest a little underripe, rather than overripe.

holding you back, keeping you from moving forward? Jesus tells us how we need to make amends with our brothers. He says in Matthew 5:23-24, "If you are offering your gift at the altar and there remember that your brother has something against you, leave your gift there before the altar and go. First be reconciled to your brother, and then come and offer your gift."

Farm gal, let's make amends with our past and resolve to do better through God's grace.

SEPTEMBER

Delayed Harvest on the Farm

He sleeps and rises night and day, and the seed sprouts and grows; he knows not how. The earth produces by itself, first the blade, then the ear, then the full grain in the ear. But when the grain is ripe, at once he puts in the sickle, because the harvest has come.

MARK 4:27-29

It was one of those harvest seasons when everything seemed to go to hades in a handbasket. (Sometimes just saying things are "hard" doesn't provide an accurate sense of the situation. So it went to hades in a handbasket. Yes, that's more fitting.)

Fields of corn were ready to be harvested. Actually, they had been ready to be harvested three weeks prior. But the corn chopper was still sitting in the middle of the field. Not chopping anything. Broken.

Farmhands were sick. Some hospitalized. Some sitting at home post-surgery. The summer seasonal laborers had returned to high school—and one, our beloved nephew Tucker, had gone on to the air force. We were shorthanded on the farm.

There was more going on too. But we won't get into all that. Just know that my usually cheerful farmer husband was tired, agitated, and trying his best not to be mad. The toil of the last several months had taken a toll.

The harvest was here—sitting out in the fields—but we didn't know when it would be harvested.

Truly, this hardness of the harvest embodies the life of most farm families come fall. Most farmers work late into the night after rising early and leaving the house before daylight. Most wives either co-labor in the fields, work their own careers without seeing their spouse, or stay at home to make sure the children are taken care of—often putting them to bed without them having seen their daddy all day.

Most of us don't naturally enjoy the feelings associated with emotional or physical toil. When hard times come, most folks instinctually just want to call it quits. But what is a farmer to do? Are they just supposed to mow down the fields and say, "Maybe next year"? No, because then nothing would be gained.

Harvest is the time to dig in your heels and focus on getting the job accomplished. You just hustle in the farm way of life and know that sleep will come in another season, your body will ache, but you have the firm resolve that you'll finish the job you started.

When the harvest is nigh, we don't stop. We ready ourselves, and we thank God that the seed grew into a harvest. Even when times get challenging, we must prepare ourselves for the challenge by not sinking into a pit of despair but recognizing the blessing of the situation.

Our harvest on the farm was eventually harvested. Sleep eventually came to the farmer and farmhands. Daddy's good-night kisses came to the farm kids. And the farmer came home to his wife.

In the end, all was well—even though we didn't know when the harvest would actually occur. God didn't desert us; He just needed us to labor through. Anything worth doing is often hard.

In our spiritual lives we can't be sure when God will reap His earthly harvest either. But we must ready ourselves, so our souls will be prepared to face the reaping. And in these modern times, when we sometimes think the entire world has gone to hades in a handbasket, we should resolve to keep spreading the good news. Dig in our heels, stand firm in the Lord, and sow seeds for Him.

Father, I know that anything worth doing is often hard. I know that digging in is part of the process. Thank You,

Father, for walking beside me, for giving me the endurance to keep pushing through, and for blessing me with the knowledge that the harvest is worth the toil. Amen.

TO THE RESCUE

My entire household, including my pregnant self, had been sick. I was exhausted from caretaking. But what should land on my doorstep? A chicken pot pie! My friend Lacey came to the rescue. This Southern comfort food is great to dig into—especially when times are tough.

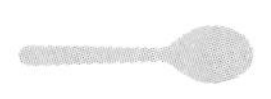

Lacey's Chicken Pot Pie

- 1 box Pillsbury pie crust (contains 2 crusts and is found in the refrigerated section of the grocery store)
- 4 boneless, skinless chicken breasts
- 1 can (29 oz.) Veg-All home-style large cut vegetables
- 1 can (8¾ oz.) whole kernel corn
- 2 cans (10½ oz. each) cream of chicken soup
- Salt and pepper to taste

Bake bottom pie crust in a deep pie dish as directed on the Pillsbury box. Boil chicken breasts until cooked. Finely slice or shred the cooked chicken into a large mixing bowl. Drain the homestyle vegetables and the corn. Discard the extra liquid. Then combine the vegetables and corn with the chicken, cream of chicken soup, salt, and pepper—stirring by hand. Pour the mixture over the bottom pie crust. Place the remaining (uncooked) crust over the mixture. Cook at 350° for 30 to 40 minutes. Enjoy!

SEPTEMBER

Letting Go on the Farm

Remember the former things of old;
for I am God, and there is no other;
I am God, and there is none like me,
declaring the end from the beginning
and from ancient times things not yet done,
saying, "My counsel shall stand,
and I will accomplish all my purpose."

ISAIAH 46:9-10

Tobacco baskets. Those are one of the top ten hallmarks of a farmhouse-style home.

For most they are a decoration purely aesthetic in nature; for us they are a decoration of remembrance. Our farm was founded on tobacco. My husband and his siblings—Marc, Gretchen, and Lauren—remember the hundreds of acres of tobacco that once grew on the farm.

They worked hard from a young age. Labor multiplied. This crop relies on hands-on labor from planting to harvesting. It isn't a crop for the weak of heart. You ask any of the older folks in our area about tobacco, and they will laugh a wicked little laugh and say they are glad those days are over. It's one of those crops that is fondest in the safe confines of memory.

Tobacco has been around North America since before it was settled by the colonists. The first commercial crop was planted in Virginia around 1612 by an Englishman named John Rolfe. Tobacco became king.

Several years into our marriage it became apparent that the cost of cultivating tobacco had become higher than the profit. My father-in-law and husband made the decision to move on from something that had been in the family for decades and decades and decades. Tobacco on our farm wasn't going to last until the end of time.

The decision was hard, because it's difficult to move on from traditions that have been in the family for a long time. Don't get me wrong—the decision was made much, much easier because we were going to stop growing a crop that had harmed many. However, questions such as "What now?" and a bit of nostalgia over bygone days were present in the decision-making process.

Change. At times it's hard to reconcile with moving forward while leaving a piece of yourself in the past, isn't it? But we can't cling to days of old just for the sake of tradition; we must make decisions based on current wisdom. This pertains to all the things we hold on to—our occupations, our family ways, our traditions.

In agriculture, markets can change, and we must be willing to meet the current needs of society. We don't always choose change—sometimes change chooses us. Standing firm on the things we know are correct is important, but we must not be so hard headed as to think that things will remain exactly the way they are now. Instead, we must be resilient.

Change can be a big type of adversity, can't it? But we must forge through this adversity with resilience and adaptability—while holding on to our core. And our core is the one who made us, the one who is the source of our personal and social stability.

In our fast-paced world we will see changes in every facet of life. However, change is made easier to handle when we stand on the firm foundation of the one who never changes: God.

God stands from the beginning to the end.

God is the one who provides us resilience, safety, and the promise of forever. We know we can bounce back from anything when we walk with Him. In an ever-changing world, the one thing we can trust will never change is the great I Am. Let's hold on to Him, not the things of this world.

HOLD ON NO MORE CHALLENGE

Farm gal, if you are like me, you hold on to more *stuff* around your house than you need. I'm currently going through boxes and boxes of clothing I'd saved. Do I need these anymore? No. But those precious little onesies bring back such memories of when my children were newborns. Only, they aren't newborns anymore. And we aren't having any more children. It's time for us to *move on* from that phase.

Even though it is hard, consider spending a day, a half day, or just ten minutes a day for two weeks discarding items you don't need anymore. You'll find such freedom in letting go of items as you embrace your present and future.

OCTOBER

Spills on the Farm

Be steadfast, immovable, always abounding in the work of the Lord, knowing that in the Lord your labor is not in vain.

1 CORINTHIANS 15:58

I have a love-hate relationship with cereal. I love that it is an easy breakfast or snack option that my children can prepare on their own. But I hate the inevitable spills that occur—usually, right after I've mopped the floor. If they can eat it, they can make a mess with it. This applies to cereal, crackers, and all food groups.

Do you ever feel like some of the tasks you do are useless? There's a constant undoing of the doings you just got done. The lawn mowing, the laundry, and even the plucking of your eyebrows. Some days you just go about your business and clean and pluck without complaint. But other days it gets to you, and you want to throw in the towel.

Sometimes work on the farm can seem to be done in vain as well.

One night during harvest season, the children and I were riding along with my husband. All of a sudden we looked out the front window of the vehicle and saw beans all over the paved road. These beans made a trail straight to our farm. Perry didn't say a word as he turned our vehicle around and hightailed it into one of our crop fields. He jumped from the vehicle, inspected the dump truck that was used for hauling soybeans, and threw his hands in the air in exasperation.

You see, back in spring we had purchased the seeds. Prepped the ground. Planted. And growth occurred. We identified a promising crop. And now we were at the end of the harvest. The part when the crop is transported by dump truck to the farm and then taken off to market.

But instead of resting in the truck, ready to be shipped to market, the soybeans were all over the road.

All over the road.

One of the farmhands had failed to latch a small piece of the tailgate, and on the drive from the field to our farm base, the soybeans spilled out. The small hole allowed a large quantity of beans to stream out, completely unnoticed by the driver.

Later I was able to point out to my kids the importance of being faithful in the small tasks, but I didn't dare moralize this startling event while we were still in the trenches of it. There is a time and place for everything—and this clearly wasn't the time or place.

The profit had been lost, but most upsetting was that all the labor that had gone into producing the crop had been done completely in vain.

As a mom, I identify with those feelings, but it's entirely different when you are out five dollars for a box of Honey Nut Cheerios and have to wet a towel and bend over to clean the floor—compared to this farming situation, where we were out all that time and labor, plus the money we'd spent to put up the crop. We were dealing with a little more than a cereal spill.

Farm gal, sometimes our work, big and small, can seem to be done in vain. In our homes. In our occupations. In our relationships with others. Thankfully we have the assurance that the work we do for the Lord is never in vain. In fact, He calls us to be steadfast and immovable.

Those cereal spills I clean up are part of making sure my kids are fed. The laundry I endlessly fold is part of making sure they are clothed. And the soybeans...well, I'm sure there's a redeeming quality in that story as well, although it's still too fresh in our minds for us to wax poetic about that particular circumstance.

But we have the promise that when we work for the Lord, nothing is ever done in vain. Although at times we want to throw our arms up in exasperation, we can instead throw them up in triumph, knowing that the Lord can take what we see as a waste of time and bless it tenfold.

I'M FIXIN' TO FIX THAT

It's not much fun to fix spills and other problems, is it? But I'm fixing to talk about something you'll want to fix right now. When you feel like you are drowning knee deep in mud—well, make some Mississippi mud. My grandmother Faye could make this with her eyes closed. It'll fix you right up.

Faye's Mississippi Mud Fudge Cake

Cake

- 1 cup (2 sticks) butter
- 2 T. cocoa powder
- 4 eggs
- 2½ cups sugar
- 2 cups self-rising flour
- Pinch of salt
- 1 T. vanilla
- 1 cup pecans, chopped
- 1 bag (16 oz.) miniature marshmallows

Frosting

- ½ cup (1 stick) butter
- 2 T. cocoa powder
- 1 box (16 oz.) powdered sugar
- Pinch of salt
- 1 T. vanilla
- Splash of milk, for thinning (if needed)

Directions for Making the Cake

Melt the butter and cocoa together on the stovetop. Cool. Add the eggs, sugar, flour, salt, and vanilla to the saucepan. Mix well. Add the nuts. (The batter will be thick.) Spread the batter into a 9 x 13-inch greased and floured pan. Bake at 350° for 30 minutes. When the cake is done, scatter the marshmallows over the top of the cake while it is still in the pan. Return the pan to the oven long enough to melt the marshmallows (but don't let them turn brown). Remove the cake. While the cake is still a bit warm, cover with frosting so the frosting melts atop the cake. Cool before cutting. Enjoy!

Directions for Making the Frosting

Melt the butter. Add the cocoa. Stir in the powdered sugar. Add salt and vanilla. Thin with milk (if needed). Stir over low heat.

OCTOBER

Pumpkin Party on the Farm

You have enlarged the nation
and increased their joy;
they rejoice before you
as people rejoice at the harvest,
as warriors rejoice
when dividing the plunder.

ISAIAH 9:3 NIV

You haven't seen joy until you've seen our best friends' kids prancing through the pumpkin patch, picking out their *perfect pumpkin*. It's pure chaos—and pure joy—to see the children swish and swash through the patch, rejoicing at the harvest. A harvest we planted with our hands and are happy to share. Happy that the pumpkin plunder can be divided among such willing harvesters.

Yes, those pumpkins we planted way back in June are finally ready for harvest. In mid-October we usually host a small group of friends for a hayride and old-fashioned pumpkin picking in our patch.

The children, decked out in full costume, jump off the trailer when we arrive at the patch and *run*. It's always funny to see which pumpkins they choose. Some gravitate toward the biggest ones, and some the smallest. Some like the white pumpkins, and some want the creepy pumpkins with the bumps. They jump over the vines and wait on their parents to bring out a pocketknife and cut the pumpkin of their choosing from the vine. Then they climb back up on the trailer, tightly gripping their plunder, and start talking about how many s'mores they will eat around the campfire.

Each season is marked by different traditions. In our home state of Tennessee, it seems like the limbs of the deciduous trees are the calling cards of each season. The barren branches of winter. The delicate, colorful buds of spring. The leafy green of summer. And then the jewel-toned leaves of fall. The Cherokee National Forest and Great Smoky Mountains that surround our homeland are frequently visited for their fall foliage. The turning of these leaves whispers the message that it is time to greet the seasonal traditions of fall. The area sparkles with radiant colors.

In the classic book *Anne of Green Gables* by L.M. Montgomery, Anne, with branches full of autumn leaves, proclaims, "I'm so glad I live in a world where there are Octobers."[1] Are you? Do you feel that joy when fall arrives? I'm truly a summer girl at heart, but I do love that fall calls for boots, flannel shirts, bonfires with s'mores, and hot apple cider.

Do you make time to indulge in your favorite fall traditions? I hope so. If not, perhaps you could make plans to do one of the following harvesttime activities. You might…

- go berry or apple picking.
- take a walk in the outdoors and admire the changing leaves.
- take a scenic drive to the mountains and breathe in the crisp air.
- break out the flannels and build a backyard bonfire.
- rake leaves and jump in the pile.

Or, if you are feeling hospitable, you could plan a harvest party. I promise, it doesn't have to be fancy. You only need three ingredients for a successful fall party: food, fire, and friends. Invite some friends over and spend an evening sitting and laughing under the stars.

I'll give you a little tip: Ask your friends to bring some food. Having others help in the food part of a gathering is rooted in rural history. To survive in any agrarian society, people have to have rugged individualism. But the communal aspect of life in the past—like barn raisings, bean stringing, and meat

WHEN IS THE PUMPKIN RIPE FOR THE PICKING?

A pumpkin is usually ripe when the vine has died, the stem is hard and dry, the skin is hard, and the coloring has reached the desired hue. It's overripe if you feel any soft places. Throw that one to the cows!

As a point of caution, when harvesting, check underneath the pumpkin for black widow spiders; they like hanging out under these orange beauties.

Use pruning shears or a knife to cut the pumpkin from the vine. You'll want to leave a long stem—at least six inches will help prevent early rotting. Also consider wiping the pumpkin with a ten-part water and one-part bleach solution. This, too, will help prevent early rotting. Enjoy cooking, displaying, or carving your pumpkin!

butchering—also played a pivotal role. Even social occasions were catered in the old-fashioned way: cooperation.

My great-grandmother, Mama Kate, always provided our favorite tradition at her fall gatherings: apple stack cake. Layers upon layers, carefully crafted with dried apples, spices, and flour. I now know that it is a monumental feat to create the cake by oneself. But for Appalachian gatherings of the past, the mountain folk didn't create these cakes all by themselves. Nope, layers would be donated by different women. Then the layers were stacked together, up to 12 layers high, for the community to enjoy at the social event.[2]

Around here I use this "apple stack cake" manner of hosting events. My friends all contribute their specialties. I can always count on Chrissi to bring desserts and Tonya to bring a delicious dip or two. That is how we craft a social gathering: cooperation. Why don't you give this a go? Then you can dig into the deliciousness that everyone creates!

REJOICING AT THE HARVEST

Fall lends itself to together time with friends and family. Whether you decide to plan a few fall outings with your immediate family or you decide to invite over a few friends and relatives for a backyard shindig, spend time rejoicing in all that God has provided.

I'm so glad I live in this world that God created. Spring. Winter. Summer. Fall. I happen to love them all, but I especially love watching my children and my friends' children build forts with the hay bales and play "king of the mountain" on the night of our pumpkin party. It's truly the simple things that bring us the most joy. God made the simple to be simply amazing.

OCTOBER

Bulls on the Farm

Do not be deceived: God is not mocked, for whatever one sows, that will he also reap.

GALATIANS 6:7

It was late fall. The weather was unusually hot for Tennessee. So my two kids, three years old and six years old at the time, took advantage of the sun and practiced their cannonballs into the pool. Wearing nothing but their birthday suits.

Then we heard sirens. Getting louder and louder.

I got the kiddos out of the pool, and we peeked around the corner of our house to find a few of our farmhands gathered. They were animatedly pointing in the direction of the front pasture. The place where our Black Angus bulls, who are bred for strength, live when they aren't out visiting the ladies of the fields.

I saw that the perimeter of the front field was flanked by police cars.

I tried calling my husband. No answer. I tried calling my father-in-law. No answer.

In that moment I realized I was the representative of the farm and needed to go find out what was happening. I loaded up my Yukon with my wet, naked kids and told them to hide in the back and wrap themselves up in towels.

Why were the police cars outside our bull pen? Well, farm gal, the story is stranger than fiction. It started with a motorcyclist eluding police. Not wanting to get caught, this fleeing suspect hightailed it off the highway and down our two-lane road.

High-speed police chases aren't usual for our neck of the woods. The motorcyclist, most concerned with the police on his tail, must have missed our "Duck Crossing" sign—and he definitely didn't see the gaggle of geese that forgot to look both ways before they attempted to cross the road.

What exactly happens when a chicken (I mean goose) crosses the road on Philpott Farms? Well, the punch line is pretty harsh. They get run over by a suspect on two wheels. But on their deathbeds, those geese got the last laugh.

As he rounded the curve, the assailant hit the geese, and his motorcycle spun out of control. While feathers flew, the motorcycle skidded off the road and wedged itself under the oak-board fence. The man then ran right into our loading zone for bulls.

Not being one to make good judgment calls, the outlaw jumped the fence and hightailed it through the pasture.

By this time the police had arrived. One of the policemen jumped from a patrol car and followed the man over the fence. Neither the suspect nor the cop realized they were in a pasture with 50 Black Angus bulls. Each one 2,000 pounds of pure testosterone. Always ready for a brawl.

Bulls are known for their ferocity toward other males and are curious about any calamity that unfolds before them. These bulls, not known for backing down from a challenge in their own pasture, weren't happy to see intruders.

To make matters worse, the criminal was wearing a red hoodie.

Unfortunately, this man was not a trained matador. He was more like an amateur rodeo clown.

Jackie, our lead foreman, recalls that he was in a neighboring pasture and saw the scene play out before his eyes. He says the policeman drew his Taser and braced for a standoff with the mob of stout animals.

Yes, a Taser.

Ever see a bull taken down by a Taser? Me either. But I've got to give him credit—he didn't turn and run. This brave man of the law stood his ground.

Jackie, very aware of the potential peril and not wanting to see an officer taken down, jumped behind the wheel of the Ranger. Jackie, now a knight in a muddy UTV, put the pedal to the metal and rushed off to rescue the policeman in distress. Jackie drove straight to the altercation, and the policeman jumped into the UTV.

Meanwhile, Red Hoodie was still trying to flee the field, but before he could make his escape, Jackie chased him down and lassoed him to the ground. (All right, he didn't actually lasso him to the ground, but wouldn't that have been a made-for-television ending to this story?) In all actuality, Jackie and the policeman (who was now riding shotgun in the UTV) apprehended him and loaded him into the UTV, and Jackie drove them all back to the safety of the roadside.

I'm still not sure if Jackie entered that bull pen to protect the bulls, rescue the policeman, or make a citizen's arrest—but regardless, you mess with the *bull*, you get the *horns* (or Jackie on wheels).

And that was when my children and I pulled into the pasture. The kids peeked through the car windows to see a handcuffed man being escorted out of the bull pen and taken to the back of the police cruiser. It was their first time witnessing an arrest—and mine too. Justice had been served for this alleged criminal who caused mayhem on the farm.

I scooted out of the pasture after finding out that Jackie was there to handle the authorities. I was afraid one of my kids, still naked from the skinny-dipping, would hop out of the vehicle and make an awkward situation even worse.

As we drove away, my kids and I had a talk about reaping what you sow. The Bible tells us that when we make bad decisions in life, we will be met with bad consequences. What you plant in life will be harvested. Thankfully God also tells us that we can repent. If we've been planting seeds that make us end up in the back of a police cruiser, we can go to God, ask forgiveness, and start planting a better crop for our lives.

This faux matador in the red hoodie taught my children an important lesson. It's one thing to be told a cautionary tale, but quite another to see it unfold before your very eyes. Handcuffs are memorable.

"We gonna pray for him," spouted out of my Southern mouth as we pulled back up to our house.

My children still talk about the day the bad guy came to the farm. And I'll always remember the day we found out what happens when a goose crosses the road.

I certainly appreciate the bulls making sure that the "No Trespassing" sign we have hanging outside their pasture is strictly obeyed. Maybe the motorcyclist will consider rule following in the future too.

I HERD THAT!

Bulls, cows, heifers, and calves. Do you know the differences between them? Once a city-slicker friend asked my husband, "How many bulls do you milk on your farm?" My husband's reply was quite humorous—I'll just let you giggle at possible responses to that inquiry. But all the terms *can* get a bit confusing. Here's some cattle lingo 101 from Farmer Perry.

- *cow*: female bovine that has birthed a calf
- *heifer*: young female bovine that has not yet birthed a calf
- *bull*: male bovine with all his parts intact, set aside for breeding
- *steer*: male bovine shed of his breeding parts
- *calf*: male or female baby bovine
- *open cow*: a female bovine that is not in calf (pregnant)
- *weaned calf*: a male or female baby bovine that no longer drinks its mother's milk
- *yearling*: a male or female calf that is a year in age (similar to how we call a young child a toddler)

Did you know that more than 70 breeds of cattle exist in the United States? The top ten (most popular or common) breeds in our country are Black Angus, Charolais, Hereford, Simmental, Red Angus, Texas Longhorn, Gelbvieh, Holstein, Limousin, and Highlands.[1]

OCTOBER

Staying Present on the Farm

You were straying like sheep, but have now returned to the Shepherd and Overseer of your souls.

1 PETER 2:25

One weekend when Beckham was a year old, we walked outside to play. Our Sophie, four years old at the time and always moving, played "castle" in the haystacks and boogied all over the wooden trailer, pretending it was her personal stage. Meanwhile, the littlest wandered among the orange pumpkins, played under the corn shocks, and chased the purring golden kitten.

I watched and smiled at their antics, enjoying the fall breeze and warm sunshine. After a while I decided to start moving the 50 or so small pumpkins sitting on the grass and place them atop the wooden picnic tables beside us. I'd pick up the pumpkins, look around to ensure the safety of my two kiddos, and then carry my armful of pumpkins to a table. My eyes would go from pumpkins to table to kids—and back again. I did this almost a dozen times.

But my phone was sitting on top of the picnic table too. And it beckoned me to pick it up. The siren call of *what I'm missing out on by looking at what's right in front of me* sang loudly, urging me to abandon my careful watch.

I picked up the phone. And started swiping toward the news to see the status of the Florida Keys and Miami as they were being battered by a hurricane. I escaped for a few brief seconds into the news story, wondering how my family, who lived close to Miami, would fare.

Suddenly, my reading was interrupted by my daughter's screams. She was on the other side of the pumpkin-filled trailer. I ran.

My heart stopped when I spotted my kids, but my legs kept going. I screamed, but internally praised God.

The one-year-old had chased the little yellow kitten all the way to the goldfish pond that sits in our yard. And my baby boy was in the pond.

His sister, the four-year-old I frequently bemoan for being too independent, was clutching the back of his footed pajamas, keeping his body from going under.

Breathe in. Breathe out.

What if Sophie hadn't been there? What if she hadn't been so independent and capable? *What if…?*

I snatched up Beckham and tucked both my kids into the safety of my lap. Tears streaming, I hugged them and told Sophie, "You saved Baby Boy's life. You *saved* Baby Boy's life. *You saved* Baby Boy's life."

And then I cursed that phone. That siren dangerously lurks and beckons us to go off course. That siren keeps many a mama and dad from fully engaging with their children.

The irony didn't escape me. You see, when we worry too much about other people's storms, we are liable to create tragic storms in our very own lives.

My baby could have drowned.

I'm the mama who is hyperalert at all times. We've had too many bad accidents in our lives for me to be anything but vigilant. But in this one circumstance I let down my guard. And my child, too young to swim, ended up in the pond.

That sentence sends shivers down my spine.

Thank You, God, for saving this child. Thank You for making sure that my capable Sophie, who loves her little brother, was on guard.

I shall heed this warning. And I share it with you too. *Put down the phone.* We must keep our attention on what is before us.

When will I try to check my phone? In the morning before everyone wakes up, in the car before I start the engine (after everyone is buckled in), while I'm cooking meals (yes, this is why my food doesn't taste as good), and at night when I have some time to myself. When my littles are around, I'm going to be more purposeful with my time.

MIND YOU

Let's worry a bit less about what's going on elsewhere and focus more on what God has placed right in front of our eyes. We can't control what is afar, but we can shepherd the sheep that are in the pasture with us.

It's easy to lose our focus on the present—and on the one who gives us presence. Sometimes our minds are like sheep and go astray. Let's bring them back to the present and rest in the presence of the Lord and those He has placed in our lives.

Heavenly Father, I pray that I will not take my gaze off You and those You have put in my care. Help me focus on showing love, support, and kindness to those directly on my path each day. Help me resolve to worry less about things out of my control and focus more on what is in front of my eyes. Amen.

NOVEMBER

One-Room Schoolhouse on the Farm

It is the hard-working farmer who ought to
have the first share of the crops.

2 TIMOTHY 2:6

About the time the muscadines are giving their final adieu in our vineyard, our rural community's harvest celebration occurs.

The harvest supper is always the first Saturday of November. We gather in the former one-room schoolhouse just up the road from our farm. The small building, crafted of brick and wood, sits in the middle of a pasture overlooking a raised hill. It's in need of a paint job, but that doesn't discourage anyone from visiting.

As we arrive we see folks sitting on the outdoor stairs. It's already dark outside, and that just makes the lights of the building seem brighter. Declaring that warmth is within the four walls.

We crowd into the room, hands holding food we've prepared, and place our contributions on the long table that is already full of roasts, baked hams, and casserole upon casserole. Laughter and stories fill the tiny space as everyone sits in the old schoolhouse desks. Toddlers and older folks and every age in between partake in the prayed blessing and the bounty of the food, everyone making certain to grab two or three or four pieces of pie and cake from the table devoted just to desserts.

And then there are the homemade fried pies. The bliss of fried pies!

This harvest supper has been going on for longer than anyone can truly remember. It is a given in our community. A marker of time and a nod to days gone by. The older generation—including the caretaker of the school, Mr. Henry and my father-in-law, Dale—remembers going to school in the very room in which we gather. Now they fondly watch their grandchildren and great-grandchildren prance across the wooden floors.

The waning of fall is a time when we tend to gather together, isn't it? To eat and be. The frantic part of the harvest has been completed, and folks can enjoy a bit of the gift of their labor.

God admires hard work, grit, and determination. And He blesses that hard work. You work hard on the farm; you should enjoy the fruit of your labor. That is the literal interpretation of 2 Timothy 2:6, which says, "It is the hard-working farmer who ought to have the first share of the crops." And I think God means it.

But we can also look to this passage as a metaphor for our spiritual lives. When we read the passage in its entirety (2 Timothy 2), we find that the author of the letter (Paul, who was imprisoned for his faith) encourages us to be like soldiers, athletes, and farmers as we become the hands and feet of Jesus and share in the sufferings of Christ.

Paul was certainly sharing in Christ's sufferings, wasn't he? Held in prison and abandoned by many whom he had thought were friends (see 2 Timothy 1). So in this letter to Timothy, his young protégé, about being strong in the faith and being a faithful giver of the Word, he was writing what he was living. A true model.

What is required of us? Paul wrote that we need endurance. Like a soldier we must be devoted to our mission and aim to please our commanding officer, God (2 Timothy 2:3-4). Like an athlete we must work hard and play by the rules of the game laid out in God's Word (see verse 5). And like a farmer we must have the mindset that diligent work will reap a harvest that we, too, will get to enjoy (verse 6).

And what is that harvest? It's the same harvest that Paul anticipated—the eternal reward of heaven, where all faithful followers will gather to enjoy the fruit of the labor.

Our community gathers on this cold November night, surrounded by the warm love of neighbors. It's quite glorious. The food. The intergenerational friendships. The memories in that one-room schoolhouse. We sit and enjoy the fruit of the labor—of the builders who constructed this schoolhouse, of those who have kept the building in good shape, and of the farmers and cooks who prepared this food for our gathering tonight.

But this night of joy after the harvest will not compare at all to the joy of heaven. The rainbows. The streets of gold. The mansions. The angels. Fruit from the vine. The gathering of all generations who join in our Christian heritage.

Farm gal, it is more than we can imagine. And we get to be citizens of that place (Philippians 3:20). We get to join the Lord of the harvest (Matthew 9:38) at His very table.

Heaven is the great gathering. The true harvest gathering. The place where we believers will go and be like the farmers—enjoying in the fruit of the labor after a lifetime of diligence.

As we leave our harvest supper on this November night, I'm filled with food and a quiet contentment at getting to take part in this small traditional event. And I'm also hoping that in heaven these same hands get to help prepare whatever food we might eat up there, because heaven will certainly be a bit sweeter with the inclusion of treats like Mrs. Shirley's fried apple pies.

HARVEST TREAT

Fried apple pies, like Mrs. Shirley makes, are a bit too advanced for my culinary prowess; however, this recipe by my friend Amber is both delicious and easy. These apple dumplings are the perfect harvest treat to take to your next fall gathering.

Grab a few homegrown (or store-bought) tart apples and get cooking!

Amber's Apple Dumplings

1 ½ large Granny Smith apples (or other tart variety)

1 (8 oz.) can of crescent rolls

2 cups sugar

1 cup (2 sticks) margarine

2 teaspoons cinnamon

1 can (12 oz.) Mountain Dew

Preheat oven to 350 degrees. Peel and slice the apples. Spray or grease 9 x 13-inch baking dish. Unroll the crescent rolls and separate each roll. Place 1 to 3 apples on each roll. Fold each roll around the apples. Place the rolls in the pan. Melt butter and sugar in a saucepan over low heat on the stovetop. Pour the mixture over the apple-filled crescent rolls. Sprinkle rolls with cinnamon and then pour the can of Mountain Dew over the rolls. Bake at 375 degrees for 30 minutes. Enjoy!

NOVEMBER

Ducks on the Farm

Let all that you do be done in love.

1 CORINTHIANS 16:14

Davy Crockett might have killed a bear when he was three (as the Disney song goes, anyway), but my Beckham Philpott can boast he killed a duck when he was four. And this, my friend, is no tall tale.

It was around sunset when my boy, unbeknownst to me, let himself out our side door. I was tidying up our basement. Getting all my ducks in a row, you might say.

The farm ducks had been a bother of late. Instead of swimming in the pond, they had taken a liking to a morning and evening dip in our pool. Why they would choose our saltwater pool over the freshwater pond bewilders me.

I'd spy the raft of ducks out taking laps and go a bit berserk. Their first swim was cute. I thought it was a one-time event. I figured they were just testing the waters and would move back to the pond. But then it became part of their daily routine.

We'd chase them. Yell at them. We even placed an alligator raft in the pool hoping that would scare them.

But these ducks were undeterred. And not afraid of a flotation device.

I started talking a bit unkindly about how I'd like to "kill those ducks." It was hyperbole. An exaggeration. Yet my youngest boy, who had just turned four, didn't quite understand figurative language. He took my wish quite literally.

Beckham, being the incredibly mama-loving child he is, decided to show love in an old-fashioned manner. By bringing me the head of my villain.

Now, around these parts hunting is a true rite of passage. Most times it involves wearing camouflage, getting up before sunrise, and using some sort of weapon. But not for Beckham. Nope, he left the house barefoot, and his sole hunting buddy was Flower, the family dog. At least he possesses his Lifetime Sportsman License, thanks to his granddaddy Doug.

You must remember that I didn't even know Beckham had helped himself out the door. I was deep into cleaning, assuming that the television had been an attentive babysitter for the ten minutes I had left my two middle kids alone.

But all of a sudden my dusting was interrupted by a dull *plod*, *plod*, *plod* sound coming from the stairs. Titus and I looked up from our work to see an out-of-breath, red-faced Beckham enter the basement. His hands were wrapped firmly around the webbed feet of a dead duck.

I was aghast. Why was a lifeless winged creature *in my basement*?

Confused. Why was *my child* holding a dead duck?

Dismayed. Why couldn't I keep *anything clean*? My stairs were now covered in feathers and blood.

There were no words. Titus and I just stared at the scene in front of us. I wanted to holler, but my child's grin was as wide as Texas. Beaming, my blue-eyed bandit said, "Me and Flower got that duck! Mama, I told Flower it was *my* duck and I was going to take it to *my* mama!"

And that he did.

His little four-year-old self had hauled this feathered gift 100 yards up a hill, then up the stairs to our side door, through the house, and down to the basement. Bless his heart, that duck was about half his size. It had taken considerable effort for him to tote his trophy into our home. It turns out he had spied the duck in our yard and went after it!

"Let's go get you a bath," I finally told him. We walked hand in hand up the feathered stairs.

I left the duck on the floor in the basement. How does one even begin to clean up that kind of mess? Plus, some tales can't be told. I wanted Perry to see this story with his own eyes.

I got Beckham into a bath and listened as he excitedly recounted his adventure. He'd heard my pleas about those pool-invading ducks and taken matters into his own hands.

After I got him dried off, we had a serious conversation about making good choices. Then I took him down the stairs to get his picture taken with the duck. Every little boy deserves a "first hunt" picture.

Beckham showed me love in the most far-fetched way. He was willing to do whatever it took to make his mama happy. Looking back, I'm thankful I acted toward my big-game hunter in love instead of hysterics.

Reacting in love can be hard, can't it? A true challenge. I don't always react well, but this time, when my son's heart was on the line, I did. With patience, love, and a gentle reprimand for his poor decisions.

God asks that we do all things in love (1 Corinthians 16:14). Love is defined for us in the famous biblical passage.

> Love is patient and kind; love does not envy or boast; it is not arrogant or rude. It does not insist on its own way; it is not irritable or resentful; it does not rejoice at wrongdoing, but rejoices with the truth. Love bears all things, believes all things, hopes all things, endures all things (1 Corinthians 13:4-7).

Farm gal, I don't know what situation will arise in your life today. (I pray it doesn't involve a dead duck.) But when something does ruffle your feathers, try to react in the way God desires—with love.

CLUTCHING MY PEARLS

Yes, it certainly can get a bit nutty on the farm. And the best nuts are those that come from our trees. In November the pecans fall off our pecan trees, and we harvest them. Pie is my favorite use for these little gems—especially chocolate pecan pie. If you feel up to it, you can also follow the "true recipe" and add a splash of bourbon for taste. This recipe is from *Baking Illustrated*.[1]

Triple Chocolate Pecan Pie

3 T. unsalted butter, cut into 1-inch pieces
¾ cup brown sugar, packed
½ tsp. salt
2 large eggs
½ cup light corn syrup
1 tsp. vanilla extract
1 cup pecans, toasted in the oven for around 7 minutes and chopped into small pieces once cooled
2 oz. semisweet chocolate, chopped
2 oz. milk chocolate, chopped
2 oz. white chocolate, chopped
1 prebaked pie shell

Melt the butter in a medium heatproof bowl set in a skillet of water maintained at just below a simmer. Remove the bowl from the skillet; stir in the sugar and salt with a wooden spoon until the butter is absorbed. Beat in the eggs, then the corn syrup and vanilla. Return the bowl to the hot water; stir until the mixture is shiny and hot to the touch. Remove from the heat; stir in the pecans. Pour the mixture into the pie shell. Evenly place all the chopped chocolate pieces throughout the pie mixture. Bake at 275°, on the middle rack, until the pie looks set, yet is soft like gelatin when gently pressed with the back of the spoon (around 50 to 60 minutes). Transfer the pie to a rack. Cool completely, at least 4 hours. Enjoy!

NOVEMBER

Blessings on the Farm

Taking the five loaves and the two fish and looking up
to heaven, he gave thanks and broke the loaves.

MARK 6:41 NIV

It's almost Thanksgiving here, and I'm thinking pretty heavily about the gathering. Not the food or decor, but the prayer. Specifically, I'm thinking about my nanna's opinion on praying.

My nanna always contributed a pecan or buttermilk pie to the Thanksgiving feast, but it was her insistence on the specific description of the Thanksgiving prayer that has become the legacy which shall forever be ingrained in my heart.

My nanna was classy. Her nails were always polished, and her hair was always perfectly coiffed (thanks to her weekly beauty-shop appointment). No one would ever have mistaken my nanna for being sloppy or indifferent. Nope, she dressed smartly and had firm opinions in life. She wasn't shy in letting us know there was a right and a wrong way to use the word *bless* before a meal.

At the beginning of each meal, we all have rituals, don't we? Especially when it comes to a holiday celebration. Have you ever sat down at a table and heard someone ask, "Will you say our blessing?"

And then heads bow, prayer commences with someone saying the blessing, and after the "Amen" everyone picks up their forks and begins eating their mashed potatoes. Or perhaps they go straight for the dessert. I'm not going to judge.

Well, this was not the process at our table. According to my nanna, the above fiasco (and I'm not talking about eating pie first) is bad manners and sacrilegious. Nanna was not shy in stating as much. You see, if someone were to ask, "Will you say our blessing?" Nanna would perk up real quick and quip, "We don't *say* a blessing; we *ask* for one. We don't have the power to bless. We can't bless God, but He can bless us." She didn't stutter one bit in that monologue. Her words were strong, slow, and deliberate.

And that was the be-all and end-all. No debate. It was kind of like asking Nanna to adjust her TV dial from Fox News to CNN—it just didn't happen. So, the wording of the question would quickly be adjusted—"Will you *ask* the blessing?"—and then we would bow our heads. No one dared open their eyes to peek in fear of the wrath of Queen Doris.

I miss Nanna. Her heart was in the right place—it just so happened that she viewed the word *bless* as a verb that can only be performed by God. She was strongly convicted in the matter. God can bless us with health, a blue sky, or children, but we cannot do the same for Him. We can pray for God to bless us, but to Nanna it would be sheer insanity for us to pray that we could bless Him.

Of course, I didn't argue with her at the time. I've waited till after her death to express my view. I think that just perhaps, just maybe, when people claim that they would like to "say a blessing," they are using the word *bless* interchangeably with *thanks*. As Deuteronomy 8:10 says, "You shall eat and be full, and you shall bless the LORD your God for the good land he has given you." In that verse, we can easily substitute *thank* for *bless*. God actually tells us to bless Him. But I'm certain Billy Graham himself couldn't have told my nanna that and have her believe him.

I'm not going to say one way of praying is better than the other. We can ask for blessings, and we can also (dare I write it?) *say* a blessing. Truly, no matter the words, the idea is the same: We should look to the heavens and give thanks to our God, who has blessed us with food to eat, a magnificent place to live, and hearts that love.

Thanks. Gratitude. Worship.

Yes, that's what we all should partake in—not just before mealtime, but constantly throughout our day.

BLESS HER HEART

I shall always secretly giggle and expect someone to be struck by lightning when they utter, "Let's say our blessing," before the meal. But it truly doesn't matter what we call our prayer. *Thanks*, *blessing*, or even *grace* all have the same end. Whatever we call it, we are looking to our Father and recognizing Him as the source of all we have and all we are.

And to that we all say, "Thank You, Father," and "Amen."

Nanna's Old-Fashioned Buttermilk Pie

- 3 eggs
- 1⅓ cup sugar
- 3 T. all-purpose flour
- ½ cup butter, melted
- 1 cup buttermilk
- 2 tsp. vanilla
- 1 tsp. lemon extract (or a bit of lemon zest and 1 tsp. fresh lemon juice)
- 1 9-inch unbaked pie crust (found in the refrigerated aisle of the grocery store)

Beat the eggs well. Blend the sugar and flour, then add the mixture to the eggs. Add the melted butter and stir lightly. Add the buttermilk, vanilla, and lemon. Beat well. Place the unbaked crust in a pie dish. Pour the mixture into the pie crust and bake at 425° for 10 minutes. Then reduce the heat to 350° and bake for another 30 minutes. Enjoy!

NOVEMBER

Thanksgiving on the Farm

You shall love the Lord your God with all your heart and with all your soul and with all your mind. This is the great and first commandment. And a second is like it: You shall love your neighbor as yourself.

MATTHEW 22:37-39

The experts recommend making Thanksgiving dinner in advance. So last night I prepared our meal.

And by prepared, I mean I turned on my laptop, visited Cracker Barrel's website, found the Thanksgiving section (turkey, dressing, rolls, two pies, and three sides), and shouted "Yes!" I then chose my time for pick-up and called it a night.

I can't even get my kids to smile at the same time for a family photo, so I for sure can't put together a three-course meal. So this year it's all about kindness to myself. A little more grace and a lot less home cooking. Yes, we are having a Cracker Barrel Thanksgiving at my house.

I have to tell you that for me the most taxing decision of all was choosing the three sides. I actually sprang for four side dishes, because who can say no to hash-brown casserole? And I shall not fib. I ordered one extra pie because it was chocolate pecan. I was sold at *chocolate*.

Now my big "job" as the hostess of our family Thanksgiving is putting the disposable cookware into the piping-hot oven and then, two hours later, sliding my hand into my Pioneer Woman oven mitt and taking out the delicious masterpieces.

Bada bing! Thanksgiving is served. And my sanity is saved.

I grew up with a lifetime of incredible homemade Thanksgiving meals. Strong emphasis on *homemade*. One holiday we had a true farm-to-table experience. One of my earliest memories is being chased by a headless turkey.

You read that correctly—*a headless turkey*. Yes, my grandparents Faye and Sam "prepared" the turkey they had raised while my brother Dustin and I watched a few feet away from the massacre. The lesson we learned was that a turkey can run without a head. I still have nightmares about that evening. I was pinned against the edge of my granddaddy's home by a turkey who ran straight toward me after the guillotine took off his head.

Farm fresh doesn't sound quite as romantic now, does it?

Other meals were thankfully not as homegrown. The Thanksgiving dinners at my late uncle David's house were always a treat. We had appetizers, drinks, yummy pecan and pumpkin pies, and all that turkey jazz. Christmas music played in the background as we filled and refilled our plates. Those are fond memories.

But with the passage of time, traditions must change, and a new host or hostess is crowned. I am now the queen of the holidays, and our relatives gather around our farmhouse table.

But there is a tiny little problem with this coronation: I am not a culinary goddess. I can't fry up okra like my grandmother Faye, carve a turkey like my uncle David, put together the best dressing in the world like my mom, mix together broccoli casserole like my nanna, or make the perfect sweet potato casserole like my aunt Melissa. In fact, I was the dishwasher and not the sous-chef at all the meals I attended growing up. And cleaning dishes, as we all know, does little to feed a hungry belly.

Alas, in this season of my life, learning how to put together a full-scale Thanksgiving feast is not something I'm willing to do. There are too many diapers to be changed, too many sibling battles to referee, and too many juices to pour. What's a mom of young ones to do?

She orders from the Cracker Barrel menu. Because she decides to be kind to herself and the rest of her family.

It was my brother's brilliant idea. He and his wife, Mary, come in from Raleigh each year, and we talked about how we wanted to actually spend time with one another. We didn't want my mom to have to spend all her time cooking, and I certainly didn't want to do that either. My dad didn't want to spend the day in line at the Honey Baked Ham Company.

After planning a trip to the zoo with all our kids, my brother—in a complete genius moment—quipped, "Sis, why don't we just get plates to go from Cracker Barrel and take them back to your house after the zoo? That way no one has to cook, and we can have more time together."

And with that one statement, he earned a "Best Brother Ever" mug, which he will be getting for Christmas.

If you are the designated host for your family's holiday feasts, please give yourself permission to be kind to yourself. If cooking up the meal from scratch makes your heart sing, go for it! If the thought of cooking the meal from scratch gives you a tension headache, call Cracker Barrel. If one year you want to do homemade, the next you want to visit the Honey Baked Ham Company, and the next you want a pizza, go for it! You are not going to set the world afire by changing things up.

This year we are having a Cracker Barrel Thanksgiving, and I'll even set up a checkerboard in our living room to provide the full-scale experience. Hot cocoa will simmer on the stove, and I'll prepare homemade whipped cream for us to place atop our purchased pies. And after the meal, instead of having to clean up a bunch of dishes, we will throw away those disposable dishes, sit around, watch the kids, eat lots of pie, and maybe play a game of checkers.

Traditions are a good thing, but don't let them ruin a good thing either. Don't become so enslaved to "the way things used to be" that you miss out on the part of the holidays that makes them truly special. It's the gathering that counts.

WHIP IT UP

The greatest commandments in life are to love God and to love our neighbors as ourselves. It's that simple. No turkey roasting required. If the best way for you to love God and others this Thanksgiving is by giving yourself the gift of takeout, do it. And if you'd prefer to show them homemade love—well, get that turkey in the oven! Whip up love, not obligation.

Thankfully, while homemade whipped cream looks and tastes impressive, it is so simple to make. Trust me. This will fancy up anything and add a touch of "homestyle" to any holiday (even if the pie is straight from the grocery store).

Homemade Whipped Cream

2 cups heavy whipping cream

4 T. sugar (powdered preferred)

Splash of vanilla

Chill a metal mixing bowl and beaters in the freezer for at least 15 minutes. Place the heavy whipping cream and sugar in the chilled mixing bowl. Add a bit of vanilla for taste. Whip together on high until stiff peaks form. Then turn the power to medium for a bit. Once the desired consistency is reached, turn off the mixer and serve the whipped cream. Goes great with fresh berries, hot cocoa, and pies. Enjoy!

⸎ DECEMBER ⸎

Royalty on the Farm

"Behold, the virgin shall conceive and bear a son,
and they shall call his name Immanuel"
(which means, God with us).

MATTHEW 1:23

This time of year, we all need a little Hallmark and a whole lotta Jesus. Am I right? Hallmark and Christmas go hand in hand. Have you ever snuggled up on your couch and devoured Hallmark Channel's "Countdown to Christmas" movies? Who am I kidding? Of course you have! Those films are hard to resist.

While watching, do you dream that you're the one walking in the winter wonderland? Ice skating. Idyllic inns. Mistletoe kisses. Christmas tree farms. Baking cookies with the most handsome man in the village. Sounds dreamy, doesn't it?

Imagine my surprise when a Hallmark movie actress and her husband moved to my neighboring town.

Of course, I was nervous the first time I met her—Hallmark stars are pure royalty in my mind. The first time Jill visited my home, I wasn't quite sure how to *entertain* a film actress. Do I get out the best china? Curtsy? Hire a violin player? Purchase a snow machine to add ambience to our event? So many decisions!

My husband said *normal* was the best policy. This translated to him grilling steaks, me inviting our friends to bring a potluck dish (I learned our royal guest is actually a fantastic cook!), and me hurriedly hiding clutter in the laundry room and making the bathrooms presentable.

After dinner everyone (adults and kids) loaded up in two UTVs for a chilly moonlight ride through the woods. Our Carhartt-jacket-clad movie star kept screaming "Faster, faster!" while Momma Sandy, McKenzie, and I sat snuggled together, praying to make it back to the house safely so we could peacefully enjoy an extra helping of Sandy's banana pudding.

Turns out that our royal guest is a country girl at heart. I had no reason to be nervous hosting her at my table. Jill and her husband, David, are easy to love. Just as easy to love as a real-deal Hallmark movie.

When we choose Christ, we all wake up in our own Hallmark-movie wonderland every day. Don't believe me? Listen up.

Your own Hallmark wonderland is filled with magnificence and glory. Look around. I bet you can see some of the splendor now. Do you see Christmas decorations that pay tribute to our King? Spy a few twinkling lights on your neighbor's house? Marvel at a night sky filled with stars? Perhaps snow is even falling from the clouds above. Yes, those are all magnificent and glory-filled sights.

But it wouldn't be a true Hallmark movie without some tension. And we all know real life is chock-full of tension. Unfortunately, struggles are promised to each of us (see John 16:33), and we all occasionally feel pulled toward a wrong decision or fall into a trial.

But just like in a Hallmark movie, our plot resolution (eternity) is a promised happy ending. For believers, everything will turn out even more perfectly than the ending of a Christmas countdown film. Yes, for those of us who follow Christ, the *happily ever after* at the conclusion of our lives is the promise of eternal life with our King.

Perhaps this is why we all love Hallmark movies so much. We watch the tension but know that in the end everything is going to turn out all right. Goodness always prevails in Hallmark movies. And goodness definitely prevails in the Bible. Check the book of Revelation if you don't believe me.

We also get to entertain royalty every single day of our lives—no nervousness, violins, or decorating required—for we entertain the King of kings, our Immanuel. He lives in our hearts and walks with us daily.

The next time you watch a Hallmark movie, snuggle up and thank God that you know a perfect ending awaits you as well. Thank Him for being with you at all times, for allowing you to be in the presence of royalty forever and ever.

HONEY DARLIN'

This cake, which my sister-in-love Gretchen frequently makes, is the ultimate companion for a Christmas visit with a friend. It pairs perfectly with coffee.

Gretchen's Honeybun Cake

- 1 box yellow cake mix
- 4 eggs
- ¾ cup cooking oil
- 8 oz. sour cream
- 1½ cups brown sugar
- 4 T. cinnamon
- 1 cup pecans, chopped (optional)
- 1 cup powdered sugar
- 2 T. honey or light corn syrup
- Hot water, for thinning

Mix together the cake mix, eggs, oil, and sour cream. Pour half of the batter into a greased 9 x 13-inch pan. Mix the brown sugar and cinnamon in a bowl. Sprinkle half on top of the batter. Swirl with a knife. Pour in the remaining cake batter. Sprinkle the remaining sugar and cinnamon mixture on top and swirl again. Sprinkle the pecans on top. Bake for 30 minutes at 350°. After taking the cake out of the oven, mix the powdered sugar, honey, and enough hot water to make a pourable syrup. Drizzle this hot syrup on top of the cake after the cake has cooled for about 5 minutes. Enjoy!

DECEMBER

Christmas Trees on the Farm

Glory to God in the highest heaven, and on earth
peace to those on whom his favor rests.

LUKE 2:14

Nothing brings about a good ol' friendly argument like the question of when you should put up your Christmas tree.

My dear friend Lacey, whom we fondly call Mrs. Claus, has Christmas music playing in the background when kids arrive for trick or treating. Once the clock strikes midnight and Halloween is over, Lacey's house turns into a sparkling winter wonderland.

My mom, on the other hand, is an after-Thanksgiving traditionalist, who also takes down her tree on Christmas night. It takes all kinds.

Research shows it makes many people happy to deck the halls early.[1] Those employees at craft stores must be oozing happiness 24-7 since they work in places that start decorating for Christmas when the Fourth of July party gear is put on clearance.

Regardless of when you put up your tree, I think we can all toast our hot cocoa to the fact that the tree is one of the best parts of Christmas. My farm home has a few fake trees and a few real ones. I put my fake ones up before Thanksgiving. The real trees are brought into our home right before Christmas. It is the search for our "real trees" that is one of my favorite Christmas traditions.

Tree hunting is a serious business. Perry, myself, and our kids bundle up in our mismatched cold-weather gear, pack an ax or two in the truck bed, and crowd into the cab of our vintage 1980s Toyota pickup. I start quoting *National Lampoon's Christmas Vacation* as we take off across our farmland in search of the perfect cedars.

The expedition takes several hours. We hike through woodlands and size up all the evergreens. Our children deliberate on which tree is the best for them. Now that we have multiple children, we end up with multiple cedars. Each child wants the opportunity to use the ax and scream, "Timber!" as their tree falls.

We load up the trees in the truck bed and haul our prizes home. (Of course, we make sure that squirrels and other creatures are out of the cedars before they cross the threshold of our house.) Then each child gets to decorate his or her tree. By the end of December our open-plan living area resembles a forest of fake and real trees.

Have you ever stopped to wonder about the history of the Christmas tree? In many ancient civilizations, evergreen boughs were hung inside homes to mark the winter solstice. These greens commonly served as symbols of life. However, it was German Christians of the sixteenth century who are credited with starting the tradition of the Christmas tree as we know it today. Legend says that Martin Luther, of Protestant Reformation fame, is credited with first putting candles on an evergreen tree. Inspired by the night sky, Luther wired candles onto an evergreen tree in his house.[2]

Historians aren't quite in agreement if this is myth or fact. However, we are certain that the Christmas tree tradition did not catch on easily in America. In fact, many Puritans cried, "Pagan!" and thought it sacrilegious of German settlers to decorate their homes for Christmas. A 1659 law was even enacted prohibiting the celebration of Christmas in the home.[3] Can you imagine?

It was in the nineteenth century that attitudes toward the Christmas tree began shifting. An illustration of the beloved royal family—England's Queen Victoria and her husband, Prince Albert (of German heritage)—surrounding their garnished tree appeared in *The Illustrated London News*, and Christmas trees suddenly became fashionable (and not sacrilegious) throughout Europe and North America.[4]

EVERGREEN

After about 500 years of Christmas trees, there still is no hard-and-fast rule about how and when to decorate for the season. However, we know with utmost assurance why God sent Jesus Christ, whom we celebrate at Christmas, and what happens when we believe in Him. That's not up for debate. John 3:16 tells us, "God so loved the world, that he gave his only Son, that whoever believes in him should not perish but have eternal life."

As we put up our trees this year, let's rejoice in our everlasting Savior who is evergreen with life. Whether our lights are white or colored, whether we put up our trees before Thanksgiving or after, and whether we go to the woods for our trees or to Walmart...we can all look at our bright trees and rejoice in our Immanuel.

CHOPPING DOWN A CHRISTMAS TREE

First, select your desired tree. You can use a saw or an ax to take it down. We prefer an ax because it requires more work and makes the event memorable for our kids.

Decide which way you want the tree to fall. On one side of the tree (the direction you don't want it to fall) notch out the tree toward the direction you do want it to fall. Then start making swings with the ax on the opposite side of the notch. Be careful not to hit yourself. Keep chopping and be ready to yell, "Timber!"

✦ DECEMBER ✦

Nativity on the Farm

Going into the house, they saw the child with Mary his mother, and they fell down and worshiped him. Then, opening their treasures, they offered him gifts, gold and frankincense and myrrh.

MATTHEW 2:11

The five-year-old awoke on a rainy, dismal Sunday and spit-shined baby Jesus. And the wise men. And Mary and Joseph. The donkeys and cattle even received this loving treatment.

Reluctance had been my state of mind when thinking about bringing up the vintage nativity set from our basement. Of all the manger scenes we own, I didn't want this one to fall victim to the negligence of my two smallest children. My 93-year-old grandmother, Faye, had entrusted me with the nativity set that our country church had used for years at our Hanging of the Greens ceremony—an evening when parishioners adorn the church with greenery and symbols of our Christian heritage. It's a service in preparation of Christ's coming. Assembling the nativity set was the centerpiece of the evening's activities.

Should I display this antique set in my home? Would it be safe in a house where sporadic sword fights and Jedi battles ensue?

After a bit of deliberation, I decided that this year I'd take my chances and unbox the much-loved relic. The contents of the well-worn cardboard box deserved to be showcased in our farmhouse, not hidden in the basement.

The dust flew as I opened the box. My Sophie helped me unwrap each ceramic, hand-painted figurine. Each piece had been swaddled with layers of cloth by the hands of my grandparents. Carefully preserved.

I'm not sure how many years it had been since the now-dusty angel had hung on top of the hand-carved barn, or how long it had been since the shepherd, now looking a bit gritty, had stood watch over the flock. But this year they were making their grand reappearance, and they needed to look their best.

The five-year-old took ownership of the task. I started getting nervous. But my hesitation turned to awe as she grabbed a nearby cleaning cloth. She sprayed a bit of cleaner on the rag and carefully scrubbed until each face shined. She inspected the cracks in the ceramic to make sure they could withstand another year. She took count to make sure all the major players of the nativity story were present.

And then she transferred the figurines, one by one, to the bookshelf my grandfather B.T. had built, and she gingerly set up the Bethlehem scene.

My daughter isn't known for always being careful or particularly reverent. Stray crayon marks have vandalized our walls. A Barbie doll might have lost a head. Sophie is the one who sings the highest soprano to induce laughter in the Christmas play. One minute our daughter might be a dancing princess, and the next minute she'll be skydiving off our couch. She's a beautiful soul, but a busy one. Her creativity can look like destruction to the casual observer. She's a mover. A doer.

Except somehow she understood, without me pointing my finger or raising my voice, that this hand-painted manger scene from her great-grandmother—well, it was special.

Consecrated.

Heavenly, one might say.

She realized that these Christmas decorations were deserving of her gentle, deliberate movements.

Sophie gave that manger and the most royal of all families her careful attention as she assembled the nativity. She grasped baby Jesus in her small hands and gave Him a spit shine to make sure He truly glowed.

The gingerbread village didn't receive this type of care. Neither did the Santa

Claus on the Christmas tree. Nor did the festive Winnie the Pooh figurine we had brought back with us from Walt Disney World. None of those beloved figures found themselves deserving of such time and attention.

Sophie knew. She, as a five-year-old, was able to differentiate between the other items in our house full of fun and joy and the manger scene—a holy symbol of our Christian heritage.

And that made me beam.

Like most parents, I second-guess myself all the time. My family had watched *The Grinch*, sung along with Bing Crosby, guzzled loads of hot cocoa, and crafted homemade ornaments. But had we put enough focus on Jesus? Were my lessons sinking in? Would my kids be able to see that it isn't the man coming down the chimney that makes Christmas meaningful, but our gratitude for the one who made the stars?

That morning setting up the nativity set with Sophie, I didn't second-guess myself. Her sincere act of love showed me that the heart of Christmas was apparent to her. The truth of Christmas was rooted in her soul. She was giving of herself. Engaged in silent worship. Spit shining the baby in the manger was her childlike tribute to the King of kings. Choosing to make the baby Jesus shine, not Santa.

It turns out that the manger scene didn't fall victim to the negligence of my five-year-old or even the two-year-old; instead, that dusty set found itself loved well by a sassy little girl who loves making glittery ornaments, baking holiday treats, and laughing at *Home Alone*. The nativity that once sat proudly in my old church found itself loved well by a little girl who hopes to receive a pink motorcycle from Santa, but who knows that Christ is the brightest *star* of our Christmas.

I suppose we had our own private Hanging of the Greens ceremony this weekend. Unexpected and unlikely. Unplanned. But it showed me that preparing our hearts and homes is just as important as preparing our churches.

O HOLY NIGHT

Many churches begin the Advent season with a Hanging of the Greens ceremony—a time when the sanctuary is adorned in anticipation of the coming of our King. Many of us prepare our homes (sometimes even before Thanksgiving!) with some of the same items. As we prepare our churches and homes, let's discuss the Christian symbolism with our families and talk about the *why* behind the adornments.

- **Wreaths:** The circle shape symbolizes the eternal love of God—without beginning or end.
- **Candles:** These remind us that Christ is the light of our world.
- **Evergreens:** These decorations show how our relationship with God is eternal. An evergreen tree doesn't lose its foliage, just like our relationship with God never withers.
- **Stars:** The twinkling stars among our decorations remind us of the star that shone that first Christmas—pointing us to Jesus.
- **Nativity:** The nativity, the manger scene that we put up in our homes, is a constant reminder of God's gift to us.

DECEMBER

Fallow Pasture on the Farm

The Lord said to Moses at Mount Sinai, "Speak to the Israelites and say to them: 'When you enter the land I am going to give you, the land itself must observe a sabbath to the Lord.'"

LEVITICUS 25:1-2 NIV

The year is coming to a close. Are you tired, farm gal? Me too.

Exhaustion wraps me in a sleepy elixir. The presents. The decorating. The people. The events. The emotions. I feel a letdown that the beauty of Christmas is over. I also dread the work left to accomplish. Taking down the decorations. Cleaning up after all the people. It's a weariness full of blissful joy—but nonetheless a tiredness that makes me want to collapse into bed for a week.

I don't have a week to recover, and I bet you don't either—no matter what season of life you are in now. But I do gift myself a day or two or three post-Christmas to not worry about the cleaning and chores. Instead, I drink coffee, read, and enjoy the crackling fire while my children play with all their new goodies. I also forgo trips to the grocery story. We've hosted enough parties for my family to be able to scavenge for leftovers.

We all need a bit of rest—mentally, physically, and emotionally—in the period after the skitter-scatter of the holidays. A time to relish the revelry. Rest restores our spiritual nutrients. When we are refreshed, we can yield a better crop.

I guess I'm a little like the fields. I need to lie fallow for a while.

I used to think that *fallow* was a type of grass or plant, like fescue or alfalfa. I'd ask my husband what was growing in a field, and he'd answer, "It's fallow."

Eventually I learned that the term *fallow* actually means "empty" or "resting." The fields my husband was referring to weren't growing anything at all. I'd totally misinterpreted his explanation. After telling him about my confusion, he explained to me that fields lie fallow to revive themselves of nutrients. The land is essentially taking a rest. A little beauty sleep.

This approach to agriculture is mentioned in the Old Testament when God speaks to Moses with a message for the Israelites. "When you enter the land I am going to give you, the land itself must observe a sabbath to the LORD," God says (Leviticus 25:2 NIV). The reasoning behind this rest was multifaceted. But one of the reasons for the land to "lie fallow" (Exodus 23:11) was agriculturally significant. Land does need a period of rest. Crops take nutrients from the soil. Time is needed for those nutrients to be revived, for earthworms to inhabit the soil, and for cattle and livestock to stomp through and add fertilizer.

Most farmers today don't follow the Old Testament protocol of a sabbath rest every seven years, but most farmers do engage in crop rotation or a seasonal rest for the fields. They know the value of respite: a higher crop yield.

Friend, every once in a while we, too, must take a little break. To be revived and refreshed. That's the season I'm in right now. After coming off a month or two of plenty and feeling a bit overworked, it is time for me to lie fallow. As philosopher John Dewey wrote, "Like the soil, mind is fertilized while it lies fallow, until a new burst of bloom ensues."[1]

Let's lie fallow for a bit in order to ready our heart and soul to burst into bloom in the new year.

Ready to be planted.

Ready to grow.

Ready to bloom and bear fruit.

Ready to shoot into the sunshine.

REST UP

Farm gal, you know what I want you to do? I want you to rest. I want you to give yourself permission to sit in your home and just be. Let those chores go by the wayside for just a bit.

As a wise woman once told me, chores will keep. Take some time to read your Bible. That's one way for your soul to be nourished. God's Word is chock-full of nutrients. Revive yourself this week by pouring some God into your soul. Let Him seep into your spirt and turn that weariness into rejuvenation.

Lie fallow. Gift yourself rest so you can go fresh into the new year.

Say What?

Here are some of the best of the best Southern expressions compiled by my friend Leah Davis.

- Can y'all monogram this?
- Quit acting ugly.
- Is my hair too big?
- I'm 'bout to jerk a knot in your tail.
- I don't have enough casserole dishes.
- Is this tacky? Shoot me straight.
- I'm ill as a hornet.
- I'm fit to be tied.
- If you need anything, just holler at me.
- Well, I'll be.
- Clutch my pearls!
- He's as mean as all get-out.
- I'll say!
- Tennessee has the best barbecue.
- North Carolina has the best barbecue.
- Yes, ma'am.
- No, sir.
- This sweet tea is sour.
- I'm mad at all y'all.
- Why would they get married during football season?
- They're as country as corn bread.
- I swan.
- Plant your beans by Easter but check the signs first.
- Ain't that a pitiful sight?
- He's all hat and no cattle.
- I'm worn slap out.
- That like to have tickled me to death.
- I didn't just fall off the turnip truck.
- I might could do that.
- I haven't seen you in a month of Sundays.
- Let's mosey on.

- Bye now, come back and see us!
- Come and sit a spell.
- You want lemon in your tea?
- Play a song with a little life to it.
- Act like you got some raisin'.
- That really gets my goat.
- That grinds my grits.
- It's coming a gully washer.
- What's got your dander up?
- Ain't you a sight for sore eyes.
- Tease that hair till it cries!
- Put your gowntail on after your bath.
- Who wants to say the blessing?
- Ain't no skin off my teeth.
- That dog won't hunt.
- Well, I never!
- I've done talked all my lipstick off.
- He got so much money, he buys a new boat every time the other one gets wet.
- Don't play in 'em church clothes!
- What time's it gettin' to be?
- Let sleepin' dogs lie.
- That's a long row to hoe.
- It ain't fittin', it just ain't fittin'.
- Key lime pie goes with everything.
- She's grinnin' like a possum.
- That will make you throw your hat into the creek.
- Pray tell.
- His corn bread ain't done in the middle.
- Pretty is as pretty does.
- That's your tale; I sit on mine.
- That's your wagon to pull, not mine.
- Who are your people?
- He has one foot in the air and one foot on the banana peel.
- It's fallin' a flood.
- You never want air in the conversation.
- The tail wags the dog.
- You may forget your manners, but people never do.
- Don't be tellin' tales outside of school.
- All in good time.

Notes

Cattle Out!

1. Henry David Thoreau, *Walden* (New York: Oxford University Press, 1999), 77.
2. *Merriam-Webster*, 11th ed. (2003), s.v. "stewardship."

Breaking Ground on the Farm

1. Charles Spurgeon, "The Sluggard's Farm," June 10, 1888, *Metropolitan Tabernacle Pulpit*, vol. 43, *The Spurgeon Center*, http://www.spurgeon.org/resource-library/sermons/the-sluggards-farm/#flipbook.

Puddles on the Farm

1. "Is It True that Cows Lie Down When It's About to Rain?" *Farmers' Almanac*, January 1, 2006, accessed July 10, 2020, http://www.farmersalmanac.com/is-it-true-that-cows-lie-down-when-its-about-to-rain-8486.
2. Ronald Wallace, *The Gospel of John* (Edinburgh: Scottish Academic Press, 1991), 71.
3. C.S. Lewis, *The Great Divorce* (New York: HarperCollins, 2001), 75.

Bees on the Farm

1. See http://bigislandbees.com.

Fireflies on the Farm

1. Henry James, quoted in Edith Wharton, *A Backward Glance: An Autobiography* (New York: Simon and Schuster, 1998), 249.
2. Thoreau, *Walden*, 89.

Planting Pumpkins on the Farm

1. John Steinbeck, *East of Eden* (New York: Penguin, 2003), 213.

The Fourth on the Farm

1. Thomas Jefferson to Roger Weightman, Monticello, June 24, 1826, in "Thomas Jefferson," *Library of Congress*, http://www.loc.gov/exhibits/jefferson/214.html.
2. Vince Staten, *Jack Daniel's Old Time Barbecue Cookbook* (Louisville, KY: Sulgrave Press, 2001), 27.

Wildflowers on the Farm

1. "Why Is Pollination Important?," US Forest Service, accessed February 3, 2020, http://www.fs.fed.us/wildflowers/pollinators/importance.shtml.

Oh, Deere!

1. "G4045—peripiptō—Strong's Greek Lexicon (ESV)," *Blue Letter Bible*, accessed December 3, 2020, http://www.blueletterbible.org/lang/lexicon/lexicon.cfm?Strongs=G4045&t=ESV.

2. "G5281—hypomonē—Strong's Greek Lexicon (ESV)," *Blue Letter Bible*, accessed December 3, 2020, http://www.blueletterbible.org/lang/lexicon/lexicon.cfm?Strongs=G5281&t=ESV.

Apple Picking on the Farm

1. Found in Elisha Greenbaum, "The Old Man and the Fig Tree," *Chabad.org*, accessed December 5, 2020, http://www.chabad.org/library/article_cdo/aid/358642/jewish/The-Old-Man-and-the-Fig-Tree.htm.

Pumpkin Party on the Farm

1. L.M. Montgomery, *Anne of Green Gables* (New York: Grosset and Dunlap, 1935), 117.
2. Mark Sohn, "Appalachian Food: Culture, History, Diversity," *Mountain Promise: The Newsletter of the Brushy Fork Institute* 12, no. 1 (Summer 2001): 4, http://4efrxppj37l1sgsbr1ye6idr-wpengine.netdna-ssl.com/brushy fork-institute/wp-content/uploads/sites/38/2016/05/Summer2001.pdf.

Bulls on the Farm

1. "Top Ten Most Popular Cattle Breeds in the United States," *AgDaily*, May 2, 2018, http://www.agdaily.com/livestock/top-10-cattle-breeds-united-states.

Ducks on the Farm

1. *Cook's Illustrated* magazine, eds., *Baking Illustrated: A Best Recipe Classic* (Brookline, MA: America's Test Kitchen, 2004).

Christmas Trees on the Farm

1. "People Who Put Up Christmas Decorations Early Are Happier, Says Expert," *Unilad*, October 7, 2017, http://www.unilad.co.uk/featured/people-who-put-up-christmas-decorations-early-are-happier.
2. "History of Christmas Trees," *History.com*, last modified December 2, 2020, http://www.history.com/topics/christmas/history-of-christmas-trees.
3. Dana P. Marriott, "When Christmas Was Banned in Boston," *American Heritage* 19, no. 1 (December 1967), http://www.americanheritage.com/when-christmas-was-banned-boston.
4. "History of Christmas Trees."

Fallow Pasture on the Farm

1. John Dewey, *Art as Experience* (New York: Perigee, 2005), 24.

Thanks, Y'all

What a year! While writing *The Growing Season,* I was also growing our family. Just last week we welcomed our darling fourth child, Stella, into the world. It's been such a sweet whirlwind writing this book while carrying her in my womb.

Dear reader, I just can't thank you enough. Thank you for picking up this book and reading my words. I'm so thrilled that you chose to invest your time in these devotions; 'tis an absolute honor! I hope you loved reading this book as much as I loved writing it.

To my editor, Kathleen Kerr, and the entire team at Harvest House, thank you for taking on this project and championing a book about the rural way of life. I'm honored to work with each of you.

To my agent, Blythe Daniel, thank you for taking me on as a client and friend. You are a pearl.

Leah Davis, thank you for collecting colorful Southern expressions and sharing them with me. I'm so appreciative of this fantastic contribution you made to this book. Bless your heart!

Brother Russ, thank you for gifting sermons that always speak to the soul.

To all the folks who contribute to work on the farm—thank you. Jackie, Anita, Charlee, Robert, Mike, Greg, Rick, Ed, Clifford, Hunter, and Jason, you've been around the longest, and we certainly appreciate your hard work and friendship. And Doug, God rest your soul, I can still hear your laughter on the farm.

To all our neighbors in our community and church, thank you for being you. For lending helping hands and for sharing food and laughter. Rural America is a special place, made extra special by folks like you.

My dear friends, I'm so glad we do life together. I'm so glad you make good food when we have get-togethers. I'm so glad our kids run barefoot together through life. I'm so glad we get one another and understand the last-minute "Hey, going to be late…still out in the field!" Whether you are my friend who lives in an "on the farm" farmhouse or in a pristine farmhouse in the middle of a subdivision…I love all of you.

To my siblings and siblings-in-love—Dustin and Mary Lewis, Gretchen and Michael McDonald, and Marc and Cathy Philpott—thank you for your love and unending support. We love you and your beautiful children: Evie, Finn, Katie, Megan, Madeline, Tucker, and Cassie.

To my father-in-law, Dale, thank you for opening your arms and farm to me.

To my mother-in-love, Ruthe—above all I will always thank you for raising your son with such a kind and generous heart. You raised him to be a wonderful husband, and you love us in such a multitude of caring ways.

To Dad, thank you for giving me a love of the outdoors and teaching me to hoe watermelons when I was younger. I had the best childhood on our family farm in Claxton.

To Mom, thank you for giving me a love of words. And for taking care of me while I was writing this book. It was awfully challenging to write a book while being pregnant and raising three children. I appreciate how you've so lovingly cared for us the last several months. Thanks to you, too, Doug for all your kindness.

Oh, my darling children—Titus, Sophie, Beckham, and Stella. I can't tell you how much I adore you. Titus, I love watching you build, explore the world (and catch the fish), and grow into such a fine little man. Sophie, I love watching you do cartwheels and beg to go work cattle with your daddy. Beckham, I love watching you dance around the house and having coffee and cuddles with you. I also love how you give us all little hugs. And Stella, we all adore our newest star. My sweets, always chase fireflies, keep on marveling at the world, and know your mama loves you more than you'll ever understand. Let's plan a big adventure together, shall we? Get out the map, and let's choose!

Last, but definitely not least, thank you to my Perry. I've been holding your hand since I was 14, and I still enjoy each and every second I spend with you.

I dedicate this book to you and all your love and sacrifice. We make quite the pair—the farmer and the philosophizer. God blessed me beyond measure when He put you into my life. I love you. A million times over. I always want to hold those weathered hands of yours. You melt my heart.

But above all, thank You, God, for gifting me this beautiful life and for helping my eyes see the truths You give us. You are of and in everything.

Sarah Philpott, PhD, is the ECPA Award-nominated author of *Loved Baby: 31 Devotions Helping You Grieve and Cherish Your Child After Pregnancy Loss*. She is a proud farm wife and farm mom of four. Visit with Sarah at allamericanmom.net, where she writes about her family, life on a cattle farm in the South, and learning to cherish God's provisions in joy and sorrow.